26 April 2019

Enjoy the book!

Best Wishes,

A Tour Guide and History of Col. John S. Mo: Loudoun County, Virginia

Written, compiled, and photographed

by

Donald C. Hakenson and Charles V. Mauro

First Edition

Donald C. Hakenson, Charles V. Mauro and Steve Sherman

©2016 HMS Productions, Inc.

www.hmshistory.com

ISBN: 978-0-692-68330-9

i

Dedication

This book is dedicated to the memory of a small band of Confederate Rangers who fearlessly followed their leader; fighting for their lives, their country and their countrymen.

This book is also dedicated to those of us today who wish to retrace the footsteps of these partisans who successfully carried out their operations in the shadow of the Union capital and earned the name of Mosby's Rangers.

And finally this book is dedicated to our wives, Carol and Nancy, who put up with us as we put this book together.

Contents

Acknowledgements

We have had the opportunity and good fortune to meet eight very special men who motivated us to attempt this endeavor with the vitality and vigor of a true Southern cavalier. Unfortunately, seven of these men have since passed away before we had ever attempted to collaborate in writing and researching this manuscript. They will never know what kind of impact they had on us mere mortals. These men had the ability to bring history to life and make it real. No historians in Virginia were more renowned as chroniclers of history or superior storytellers or writers concerning their craft. They all were accomplished authors and men of immense integrity. We will miss them because they taught us how to research and not give up on the story plot until all sources of information had been exhaustedly searched. They made Virginia history fun, interesting, exciting, and enjoyable. Their names are forever etched in our memories. We hope one day Virgil Carrington (Pat) Jones, Jim Moyer, Mayo Stuntz, John Gott, Kenneth Stuart McAtee, Stevan F. Meserve, and John Divine will find out how much we truly admired and respected them.

Pat Jones' book on *Ranger Mosby* gave us our first taste of the exciting excursions of the Gray Ghost. Jim Moyer, Mayo Stuntz, Stevan F. Meserve, and John Divine were men who liked to visit the battlefield, skirmish sites and homes of Union and Confederate soldiers, and ensured that this information was well documented for the future historian. They were resident experts of Colonel Mosby, his operations, the exploits of Mosby's daring men, and Northern Virginia. All of these historians published books and articles that ensured that the operations of the Forty-third Battalion Virginia Cavalry or Mosby's Rangers was not overlooked or forgotten. They will be missed by far more knowledgeable people than us because they made the world a lot nicer place.

Dr. Kenneth Stuart McAtee instilled in us the importance of the fable, especially the anecdote that must be preserved, nurtured and never forgotten. His knowledge of Colonel Mosby and his three books on *Ghost Stories and Legends from the Old Confederacy* are a must read for everyone.

Another historian and author who motivated us by his true love for history was the indefatigable John Gott, or sometimes referred to as "Mr. Fauquier County." No man knew more about early Virginia families or had a greater zeal in describing the scene down to its minutest detail better than John. His superlative memory and knowledge of Fairfax and Fauquier counties, The Plains and Marshall made him a living legend in the academic and history field. His help, advice, and friendship were extremely valued by us. All of these esteemed men of letters are deeply missed by the authors.

Also, no one person helped us more than Thomas J. Evans. He inspired, motivated, and provided insights, recommendations, and suggestions that ensured that everything was written in grammatically correct form, well defended and backed up by historical fact and documentation.

His ability to edit this manuscript and check the facts to ensure its accuracy inspired us to complete this work of love. We will never be able to adequately thank him for his diligence, patience, and assistance. Tom Evans is a historian who is detail oriented and is a noted expert of Colonel John S. Mosby, his men, and his combat operations in Mosby's Confederacy, the State of Virginia and Southern history. We will never be able to repay him for his special assistance and his general overall kindness.

This civil war tour book encompassing the area of Loudoun County, Virginia is a testament more of his knowledge and writing abilities than of us. Tom opened up his extensive archives for us which greatly assisted in the making of this book. In addition, Tom Evans teamed up with Jim Moyer to write one of the best tour guides ever written regarding Mosby's Confederacy that highlights the roads and sites of Colonel John Singleton Mosby. Tom and Jim's five other books titled, *Mosby's Vignettes* are valuable collector's items if you can find them. Tom has also been the primary mentor to both of us in conducting the ever-popular Mosby bus tours that made him and Jim Moyer universally famous. Again, no one helped us more in the development and creation of this book than Tom Evans. We will be forever in their debt. No more gentler and nobler person has ever walked upon this earth.

A special thanks also goes to Kathleen Estes for her editing and valiant attempt at improving our English.

Additional Acknowledgements

Local historians know local history. The story of Confederate Colonel John Singleton Mosby's Combat Operations in Loudoun County, Virginia, would not have been possible without the extensive years of research, knowledge and writing of various local experts. This book is based upon the knowledge of these other eminent historians.

Wynne C. Saffer possesses a keen memory for all things Mosby and all things Loudoun County, Virginia. His has written various books and articles on Loudoun County, Virginia and has taken the reins from John Divine as the most knowledgeable historian of that county. The authors are truly indebted to him for invaluable assistance on this manuscript.

Rich Gillespie, the Executive Director of the *Mosby Heritage Area Association,* has answered many of our questions and personally taken us out on trips whenever we called to help us verify locations for this book.

Eric Buckland has spent years researching Mosby and his Rangers. Among his publications are four books aptly titled, *Mosby's Men, Mosby's Men II, Mosby's Men III, and Mosby's Men IV.* Eric has also provided many images of Rangers from his personal collection.

Special thanks also go out to Jim Lewis and David Goetz for their knowledge of John Singleton Mosby and various locations in Loudoun County.

We also need to give a personal thank you to those who allowed us access and to take photos of their private residences, both inside and out. They are Richard and Sherrie Schroeder at Miskell's Farm, Robert Feierbach at *Temple Hall*, Childs Burden at the George Dodd house, Gayle and Thomas DeLashmutt at *Oak Hill*, Donald Brennan at *Llangollen*, the Belmont Country Club at Belmont Manor, Eleanor Adams at Flemon Anderson's house, and The National Beagle Club at James Gulick's house.

Additional thanks goes to Arthur deButts for his access and photos of the bullet taken from Ranger John deButts. We want to thank Jean Forbes for the information on Isaac B. Anderson.

We are honored to compile the stories of Mosby's Rangers in Loudoun County from these exceptional local historians. They provided us the absolute best stories on the raids, the men, and the locations of Mosby's Combat Operations in Loudoun County, Virginia.

We also couldn't have done this book without our graphics designer, Stephen Wolfsberger, who added his own extensive knowledge of the Civil War and Loudoun County and translated it all into our cover design and map.

Additionally, we would be remiss if we did not sincerely thank Hugh Keen and Horace Mewborn for their invaluable comments and expertise in the development of this book.

Furthermore, we the authors want to thank Steve Sherman, President, HMS Productions, Inc., for his belief in us as researchers and authors and supporting the publication of this labor of love.

The authors also want to thank the following people for their knowledge, support, and encouragement over the many years while researching and documenting Virginia history: Mary K. Hakenson, Robert & Kelly Hakenson, Matt Estes, Susan Gray, Steve Patchan, Robert Swartwout, Bruce Dupee, Gary Buzbee, Robert J. Hickey, the late great Edith Sprouse, John Ward, Brian Buntain, John Berfield, Lewis Leigh, Susan Hellman, John McAnaw, Mark Trbovich, Edward T. Wenzel, John M. Souders, Taylor M. Chamberlin, Ken Fleming, William Gregg Dudding, Edward C. Trexler, Ted Ballard, Ben Trittipoe, Carl Sell, Phyllis Walker Ford, Patty Young, Brian Conley, Suzanne S. Levy, Anita Ramos, William Page Johnson II, Wendy Kilpatrick, Robert L. Sinclair, Al & Cheryl Kellert and Amy Payette of the Gray Ghost Winery, Maston Gray, Kim Holien, Richard Crouch, the late historian Peter A. Brown, Virginia Morton, John Kincheloe, Harper & Jackson Duong, the Stuart-Mosby Historical Society, and the staff of the Thomas Balch Library, in Leesburg, Virginia.

In closing, the authors truly appreciate everything everyone has done and hope the reader will enjoy our second manuscript as much as we did writing the first one. Finally, if the reader should discover any errors, mistakes or omissions in this vignette, they are absolutely the sole responsibility of the authors.

About the Authors

Don Hakenson has spent countless years researching obscure Civil War incidents and sites in Northern Virginia. For over a decade, Don has conducted "Mosby" tours following in the footsteps of Tom Evans and Jim Moyer. Two of Don's books, *This Forgotten Land*, which won the Nan Netherton Award, and *This Forgotten Land, Volume II, Biographical Sketches of Confederate Veterans Buried in Alexandria, Virginia,* attest to his unique knowledge of the Civil War and the men who served in it. Don has also published three other books about Colonel John S. Mosby and his men.

Chuck Mauro has researched and written extensively about Civil War history in Northern Virginia. His books include *The Civil War in Fairfax County: Civilians and Soldiers*, and *A Southern Spy in Northern Virginia: The Civil War Album of Laura Ratcliffe*. Chuck also won the Nan Netherton Award for *The Battle of Chantilly (Ox Hill): A Monumental Storm* and numerous awards for his film *The Battle of Chantilly (Ox Hill)*.

Don and Chuck collaborated on the first book of this series *A Tour Guide and History of Col. John S. Mosby's Combat Operations in Fairfax County, Virginia*. In 2015 Don and Chuck were also named Northern Virginians of the Year by *Northern Virginia Magazine*.

Don Hakenson

Chuck Mauro

HMS Productions, Inc.

www.hmshistory.com

Introduction

This book is your tour guide to over 100 locations in Loudoun County where Colonel John Singleton Mosby conducted his raids during the Civil War. It is also a guide to the locations of the historical markers dedicated to those raids and to the whereabouts of the majority of the graves of Mosby's Rangers buried in Loudoun County. We have also included a few significant military engagements that did not involve Colonel Mosby or his men as the authors felt these events should be included in order to better tell the story of the Civil War in Loudoun County.

Overall, this book is the second in a series of future books dedicated to following the plume of Mosby and his men. The first book detailing Mosby's Combat Operations is entitled *A Tour Guide and History of Col. John S. Mosby's Combat Operations in Fairfax County, Virginia,* was published in 2013 by HMS Productions, Inc.

The story of Mosby's Combat Operations in Loudoun County is about a band of Confederate cavalrymen known as the Forty-third Battalion of Virginia Cavalry, or Mosby's Rangers. This unit conducted military combat guerilla operations into Northern Virginia, behind enemy lines, especially in Loudoun County. This unit is recognized by the U.S. Army and the Marine Corps as the most feared and successful guerilla unit in the history of American warfare.

The commander of this partisan unit was a man by the name of John Singleton Mosby. He would obtain the rank of Colonel and become one of the most notorious and romantic figures that came out of the entire Civil War. He was one of James Ewell Brown "J.E.B." Stuart's men, and it was due to the confidence that General Stuart had in him that he was able to organize and lead this famous band of Rangers.

This little body of a few hundred men, under his skillful and daring leadership, accomplished more with less. The Rangers struck quickly, gobbling up horses, men, supplies and disappearing into the mist before reinforcements or help could arrive. These men yielded more trouble for the Union Army than a brigade or division could produce. They kept large numbers of Union troops guarding the city of Washington instead of fighting against Robert E. Lee in the field.

Before the war started, Mosby was a struggling young lawyer in Bristol, Virginia, a quaint little town which stands on the border line of Tennessee and Virginia, half in one State and half in the other. He was pro-Union, but when Virginia seceded, Mosby realized he couldn't fight against his mother's state. He promptly enlisted as a private in the Washington Mounted Rifles which would later be incorporated into a company of the First Virginia Cavalry. Colonel J.E.B. Stuart was commanding this unit at the time.

Mosby fought at the first battle of Manassas and at the end of the first year of the war had been promoted to adjutant in the Washington Mounted Rifles. He served under Captain William "Grumble" Jones. It was under Jones that Mosby learned to love going out on scouts and serving on outpost duty. During this time, Mosby also read and studied books on military strategy and tactics. Unbeknownst to Mosby, he was being schooled for the work that would later make his name a household word by Southerners and Northerners alike.

In late April 1862, Mosby joined General J.E.B. Stuart's staff and would become one of his most trusted scouts. In a lot of ways he was becoming a protégé of his great chieftain, Stuart. On December 30, 1862, Mosby finally received permission from Stuart to form an independent command. The rest would be history.

From January 1863 to April 1865, Mosby would conduct some of his most famous and significant combat operations against the Union forces operating in Loudoun County. Entire brigades were sent after him and a price was placed on his head, but he was always able to give his pursuers the slip. Mosby was never caught, and the bounty was never paid!

This book is just the starting point for your journey into history. It is a guide to locations you have probably passed without realizing their historical significance. Very few of these historical locations are actually marked. Many are now occupied by buildings, occurred at modern intersections, along a forgotten stream, or are now just a patch of grass alongside a road. All however, are as important today as they were over 150 years ago.

Although these raids and their descriptions are listed in chronological order to preserve their historical context, they can be visited in any order, starting and ending in whatever amount of time is allocated to each day's explorations. A current map or GPS navigation device truly allows one to explore them at one's convenience.

Here are the stories of those engagements, the locations, and the men involved in those fights. Time is yours. History is waiting for you. Enjoy!

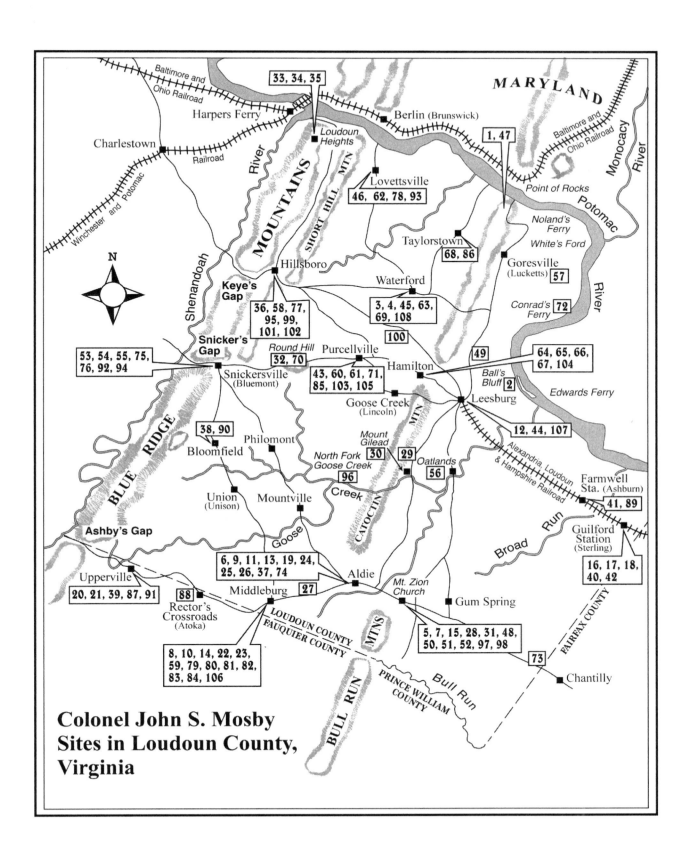

**Colonel John S. Mosby
Sites in Loudoun County,
Virginia**

3

Loudoun County Sites, Locations and Historical Markers

1) First Confederate soldier killed in Loudoun County, Taylorstown
2) Clinton Hatcher at the Battle of Ball's Bluff, Leesburg
3) Fight at Waterford Baptist Church, Waterford
4) Samuel Means House and Mill, Waterford
5) Mosby fight at the Matt Lee House, Aldie
6) Mosby's receives his first nine Rangers at *Oakham* Farm, Aldie
7) Mosby meets men at Mount Zion Church, Aldie
8) Mosby attacks Colonel Sir Percy Wyndham, Middleburg
9) Mosby visits Matt Lee House, Aldie
10) Mosby asked to stop his guerrilla operation by the citizens of Middleburg
11) Six rangers caught dancing, Aldie
12) Ball's Mill, Leesburg
13) Mosby attacks Union Major Joseph Gilmore, Aldie
14) Mosby at Lorman Chancellor House, Middleburg
15) Mosby stops at Ball's Mill and Nat Skinner's House, Aldie
16) Mosby surprised by the First Vermont Cavalry at Miskell's Farm, Sterling
17) Broad Run Toll House and Bridge, Sterling
18) Approximate location of Mr. Henry Green's House, Sterling
19) Union cavalry capture three Rangers, Aldie
20) Fight at Blakely's Grove, Upperville
21) *The Maples*, Upperville
22) Rangers captured, Middleburg
23) General J. E. B. Stuart met Major Mosby and his men in front of the Red Fox Inn, Middleburg
24) James Gulick's home, National Beagle Club, Aldie
25) Mosby captures Major Sterling and Captain Fisher at the Almond Birch House, Aldie
26) Battle of Aldie Memorial, Aldie
27) Mount Defiance. Site of Fighting between Aldie and Middleburg
28) Death of the New York Herald Correspondent, Aldie
29) *Oak Hill*, Leesburg
30) Sutler's Wagon Raid – Mount Gilead, Leesburg
31) Fight with Second Massachusetts Cavalry between Matt Lee's house and Mount Zion Church, Aldie
32) *Woodgrove*, Round Hill
33) Failed night attack Loudoun Heights, Major Henry Cole's Headquarters, Loudoun Heights
34) Failed night attack Loudoun Heights, Picket Post, Loudoun Heights
35) Failed night attack Loudoun Heights, Highway Marker, Loudoun Heights
36) Levi Waters House, Hillsboro
37) Union deserter Pony Ormsby captured by Second Massachusetts Cavalry, Aldie
38) Mosby attends a wedding at Johnson's Chapel, Bloomfield
39) Second Fight at Blakely's Grove, Upperville
40) Engagement at Second Dranesville, Anker's Shop, Sterling
41) Belmont Manor House, Ashburn
42) Guilford Station, Sterling
43) Shootout at Locust Grove, Purcellville
44) Ranger John deButts wounded in Leesburg
45) Sergeant Charles B. Stewart wounded by John Mobberly, Waterford
46) Mosby skirts Berlin (Brunswick Bridge), Lovettsville
47) Mosby fires his artillery piece "Potomac," Taylorstown
48) Mount Zion Church Fight, Aldie
49) Mosby dines at Temple Hall, Leesburg
50) Yankee Davis House, Aldie
51) Samuel Skinner House, Aldie
52) Lenah Farm Lane, Aldie
53) Mosby attacks Union wagon train in Snickersville
54) Fight against the Eighth New York Cavalry at Mount Airy, Bluemont

55) Mosby divides money after Greenback Raid, Ebenezer Church, Bluemont
56) Mosby purchases his horse "Coquette" at Oatlands Plantation, Leesburg
57) Ranger Richard Montjoy killed at Goresville, Goresville
58) Results of the Union burning raid, Potts Mill, Hillsboro
59) Results of the Union burning raid, Sally's Mill, Middleburg
60) Results of the Union burning raid, White Pump Marker, Purcellville
61) Results of the Union burning raid, White Pump Tavern, Purcellville
62) Union deserter "French Bill" Loge captured, Lovettsville
63) Mosby's men kill Sergeant Flemon Anderson, Waterford
64) Last combat in Loudoun County, Hamilton
65) Possible house where Union Lieutenant John H. Black was treated, Hamilton
66) Harmony Church, Hamilton
67) Manassas Gap Railroad Marker, Hamilton
68) Downey's Mill and Stillhouse, Taylorstown
69) Formation of Company H, Forty-third Battalion Virginia Cavalry, North Fork
70) Isaac Burns Anderson House, Round Hill
71) The killing of Confederate John Mobberly, Purcellville
72) Conrad's Ferry/White's Ferry, Leesburg
73) Mortimer Lane captured by Union troops, Chantilly
74) Snickersville Turnpike Marker, Aldie
75) Bluemont Historic Village Marker, Bluemont
76) *Old Welbourne*, Bluemont
77) Mosby's men play cards in Hillsboro
78) Lovettsville Civil War Marker, Lovettsville
79) Stoke, Middleburg
80) Mosby's Hill, Middleburg
81) *Mosby Spring Farm*, Middleburg
82) *Welbourne*, Middleburg
83) The War Horse monument, The National Sporting Library & Museum, Middleburg
84) Ranger George Dodd House, Middleburg
85) Hibbs Bridge & Marker, Purcellville
86) Loudoun Rangers lived in Taylorstown
87) *Rose Hill*, Upperville
88) Goose Creek Bridge and Marker, Atoka
89) Dick Moran Cemetery, Ashburn
90) Bloomfield
91) *Llangollen*, Upperville

Mosby's Rangers buried in Loudoun County Cemeteries
92) Ebenezer Church Cemetery, Bluemont
93) Lovettsville Union Cemetery, Lovettsville
94) *Old Welbourne* Cemetery, Bluemont
95) Salem Church Cemetery, Hillsboro
96) North Fork Church Cemetery, North Fork
97) Mosby's Rangers buried at Mount Zion Baptist Church, Aldie
98) Members of the Thirteenth New York Cavalry and the Second Massachusetts Cavalry buried at Mount Zion Baptist Church, Aldie
99) Arnold Grove Cemetery, Hillsboro
100) Catoctin Free Cemetery, Hillsboro
101) Ebenezer Church Cemetery, Hillsboro
102) Hillsboro Cemetery, Hillsboro
103) Ketoctin Church Cemetery, Purcellville
104) Lakeview Cemetery, Hamilton
105) Saint Paul's Church, Purcellville
106) Sharon Cemetery, Middleburg
107) Leesburg Union Church Cemetery, Leesburg
108) Waterford Union Church Cemetery, Waterford

Loudoun County Sites, Locations and Historical Markers

1) First Confederate soldier killed in Loudoun County on August 5, 1861 – Lovettsville Road at Furnace Mountain Road, Taylorstown

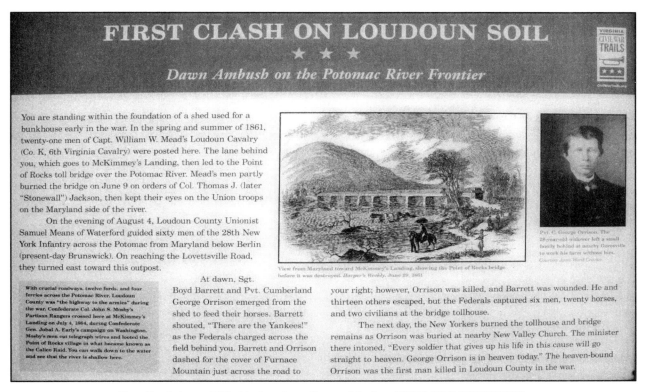

First Confederate Killed in Loudoun County Marker (N39°16'15" W77°32'56")

A sharp skirmish took place early in the war in Virginia on Monday morning, August 5, 1861, opposite the Point of Rocks Maryland at Potomac Furnace, in Loudoun County. A detachment of sixty men of the Twenty-eighth Regiment of New York Volunteers, stationed in Maryland under the command of Union Lieutenant Colonel Edwin F. Brown, crossed the river at Berlin on August 4, 1861 the night before, and marched six miles through Loudoun County and came upon a party of Captain William W. Mead's Confederate Loudoun Cavalry (Company K, Sixth Virginia Cavalry), consisting of twenty-one Confederate cavalrymen, opposite the Point of Rocks. The confederates had been on duty all night scouting the Virginia mountainside and had just arrived back to camp to rest. The Union detachment was guided by Loudoun County native Samuel "Quaker Sam" Means.

The Union colonel with his party came upon the tired Confederates about sunrise. Some of the Confederates had already fallen asleep while others were feeding their horses, and a few of the Confederates were making and eating breakfast. Lieutenant Brown ordered the surprised

Southerners to surrender which was not obeyed. The New Yorkers then fired a volley routing the Loudoun County boys, killing one, wounding two, while capturing six soldiers, two civilians and twenty horses with their equipments.

Fourteen of the Confederates succeeded in making their escape and reaching Leesburg, though they reported that the bullets of the two flanking columns whistled around them in a manner that was anything but agreeable. One of the Confederates, Boyd Barrett, had his pistol in his hand at the time of the surprise attack when an enemy minnie ball broke the ramrod and very slightly injured his hand, perhaps saving his life.

The Union infantrymen brought the captured Confederates into camp later that morning about ten o'clock without a single man in their own unit getting hurt. The only Confederate who was killed was identified as Cumberland George Orrison of Loudoun County who was shot thru the head and arm. Orrison was known by everyone who knew him as George Orrison. The Confederate prisoners were brought to the Point of Rocks by Union Lieutenant Colonel Brown, and each had an interview with General Brooks, who remanded them to the charge of Brigadier General Thomas. The names of six of the Confederates were Privates Robert Drane, Arthur Dawson, Mahlon Myers, James W. Daniel, Jonah Orrison, and George Davidson. They claimed to be privates in the Home Guard of Virginia and represented themselves to be farmers, storekeepers, and other assorted occupations from within Loudoun County.

George Orrison, First Confederate Soldier killed in Loudoun County

George Orrison's body was recovered by his friends. Samuel Houser, postmaster at Potomac Furnace, and his step-son Wade, the ferryman at that point, were likewise taken prisoners by the Union soldiers and carried to Sandy Hook, Maryland. Towards evening, Mr. Houser was released and sent home with instructions, however, to evacuate his house at once as it was the Union purpose to destroy it on Tuesday.

Andrew Morman stated after the war that George Orrison was at his father's house eating supper the night before the attack. Morman's father wanted Orrison to stay all night, but he said, *"No, Mr. Morman, I have got to go to camp."* They were camped at the tollhouse bridge opposite Point of Rocks on the Virginia side. The bridge was burned later in the day after Orrison had been killed.

Andrew had never seen a "Yankee," but they came along his house about daylight saying they were going down to capture the picket post at the bridge, and as Morman was only a fourteen year old boy, he got up, put on his clothes, and followed on down behind the Union men, about a quarter mile, when the Unionists began to fire. Later Morman said he went up to the tollhouse where Mr. and Mrs. Houser came out on the porch and said to Morman, *"There lays poor George Orrison in the road, right where the Taylorstown and Lovettsville road comes together, right at the end of the Houser barn."*

After everything got quiet, six men put Orrison on a blanket, one at each corner and two in the middle, and carried his body into the office at the tollhouse where the body remained until the citizens notified his people. Then Orrison was taken to the nearby Valley Church near Lucketts and laid about fifteen feet from the gate entering in the graveyard, where a good many of the Orrisons are buried.

A man serving with George Orrison said about the funeral, *"Elder Furr preached the funeral sermon. I shall never forget one of his expressions. It was 'Every soldier that gives up his life in this cause will go straight to heaven.' He raised his voice and said, 'George Orrison is in heaven today.' I believe as the elder did and in the four years of conflict his words of assurance were a great comfort to me. I have the hope and the belief that I shall meet him there and all the hosts of saints that have gone before me."*

Such was the belief of the men fighting for their souls during the Civil War in Loudoun County, Virginia.

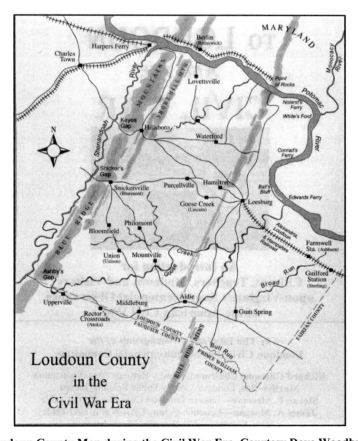

Loudoun County Map during the Civil War Era. Courtesy Dave Woodbury

2) Clinton Hatcher at the Battle of Ball's Bluff on October 21, 1861 – Ball's Bluff Road, Leesburg

Thomas Clinton Lovett Hatcher

20 December, 1839 – 21 October, 1861

Standing over 6'4" and wearing a full red beard, Clinton Hatcher was a memorable figure. Despite his Quaker upbringing, he joined Company F of the 8th Virginia at the beginning of the war and became the regimental color bearer. This combined with his height and notable beard to make him quite a target and he was, in fact, killed during this battle. This memorial stone was placed here to honor his courage. Hatcher is not buried here but rests in the Ketoctin Baptist Church Cemetery near Purcellville, Virginia, a few miles west of Leesburg.

Ball's Bluff Battlefield Regional Park

Clinton Hatcher Marker at Ball's Bluff (N39°7'49" W77°31'51")

Tom Richards, later the Captain of Company G of Mosby's Forty-third Battalion Virginia Cavalry, wrote of an incident of uncivilized warfare practices by the enemy in Loudoun County at the battle of Ball's Bluff prior to Mosby forming his independent command. He wrote:

"At that time I was a noncommissioned officer in Carter's Company of the Eighth Virginia Infantry, Colonel Hunton commanding. On this morning of the battle we were engaged with the enemy at the crossing of Goose Creek, on the Leesburg and Alexandria Turnpike. In the afternoon we were double-quicked to the woods skirting Ball's Bluff, and formed in line of battle a short distance from an open field in our front.

Our skirmishers, of which my chum Joe Calvert, also later a Mosby Ranger, and myself were members, developed the

Mosby Ranger Captain Tom Richards

enemy strongly posted in a ravine that crossed this open field, supported by a battery of artillery. We reported the situation to our colonel, and he immediately lined us up for a charge. In the meantime a Mississippi regiment had joined us and were lying down a short distance in our front. At the command we went forward, passed over the Mississippi regiment into the field at a double-quick, and went at them with a yell, the Mississippians supporting us.

The Federals did not wait to receive our charge, but broke for the river and bluffs. We followed close, crowding them down to the river bank. As we advanced to the bluff, Calvert and myself still together, came upon a pile of Federal knapsacks and a Federal soldier guarding them. He shot at us and turned to run.

Both of us were out of ammunition, but Calvert drew a pocket pistol and fired just as the Yankee reached the bluff. He struck his man, who leaped over the bluff and fell in the forks of a tree, where he lay dead until the next day. The battery composed of brass guns, was near the pile of knapsacks. Calvert and myself went up to look at them.

It was then getting dusk. As we stood there, Calvert looked down the incline of the bluff and saw a column advancing in line of battle. He called out: 'There come the Yankees.' I looked and saw the column, but in their center and front was the tall and unmistakable form of Clinton Hatcher, one of our regiment, and the soldier accredited...with the killing of Colonel Baker.

He was six feet seven inches tall, and I knew him well, as we were both students at Columbian College, Washington City, when the war began. I said to Calvert: 'They are not Yankees, for there is Clint Hatcher among them.'

We continued our examination of the guns, when the advancing column fired at us. I started on a run to my regiment, about two hundred yards back, which I reached and reported what I had seen. We were ordered forward,

Clinton Hatcher, Eighth Virginia Regiment

and met this Federal column just at the top of the hill, when there was most terrific fighting for a few minutes. The Federals again fell back to the bank of the river. This was the last fighting.

After the battle I was walking over this part of the field, when I saw the form of a very tall soldier lying on the ground with his face upward. I stooped down, and saw at once that it was Clint Hatcher. A Mississippian told me that in the earlier part of the fight he was captured, and that the Union infantry also captured a tall Virginian, and in this last charge they put himself and this Virginian in front of their column. My information leads me to believe that the Union Colonel Baker was killed in this last charge. If so, he paid with his life the penalty for the cowardly act of placing Confederate prisoners in front of his charging column.

9

Referring to Clinton Hatcher, I may mention an incident that occurred just before the firing on Sumter. We were students at Columbian College, on Fourteenth Street, Washington City. One night Hatcher and J.C. Salsby of Mississippi ran up a Confederate flag on the mast over the college building.

The flag floated there for several hours in plain view of the capitol building and the President's mansion, before it was discovered by the college officers, when Dr. Samson, the President of the college, removed it. It is doubtless the only time a Confederate flag ever floated over a public building in the Federal capital. Hatcher was a brave and fearless soldier, and had his life been spared would have won distinction in the cause for which he so early died."

Ball's Bluff overlooking the Potomac River

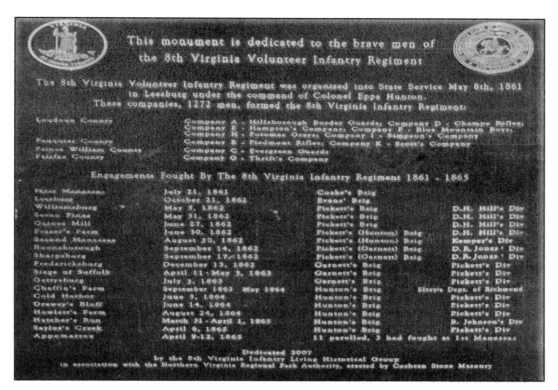

Eighth Virginia Infantry Marker at Ball's Bluff

Clinton Hatcher Stone Marker at Ball's Bluff

3) Fight at Waterford Baptist Church on August 26-27, 1862 – 15545 High Street, Waterford

Waterford Civil War Marker (N39°11'10" W77°36'38")

On the night of August 26, 1862, Captain Elijah Viers White formed his men; consisting of about twenty of his Thirty-fifth Battalion Virginia Cavalry, augmented with about thirty troopers from other cavalry units, with Captain Robert Randolph of the Black Horse Troop. They made their way outside the quaint little town of Waterford, Loudoun County, Virginia in an attempt to surprise the Loudoun Rangers, a Union cavalry unit commanded by Samuel "Quaker Sam" Means.

At dusk, the little force led by local residents Henry Ball and J. Simpson along with other civilians in the area marched across farm fields, dense woodlands, through other obstacles riding into Waterford, passing along the mountain all the way, and arriving at Franklin's Mill an hour before daylight. A halt was ordered, and various scouts were sent out to ascertain if any changes had been made in the disposition of Means' command.

Captain Elijah Viers White, Thirty-fifth Battalion Virginia Cavalry

While lying and hiding outside of Waterford, a party of eight was heard passing the road from Leesburg, who, from their conversation, was a Union scouting party that had been out all night trying to learn the movements of the Southern army. As a matter of fact, the leader of this scout was heard declaring, *"There wasn't a rebel soldier north of the Rappahannock."*

As soon as this party passed beyond hearing, White moved his people to Mr. Hollingsworth's barn-yard, which was about one hundred yards distance from the Waterford Baptist Church. White had twenty of them dismount and ordered them to march to the enemy's quarters. These men were instructed not to fire until they entered the house, or, in case the enemy was outside, to get into the yard with them before firing, and then to rush upon them. White held the remainder of his men mounted and rode to the brow of the hill in the road by Hollingsworth's gate to wait for the first movement by the dismounted cavalry to drive the Yankee boys from their quarters. White's mounted cavalry would then dash down and capture them.

At the early morning dawn, when the dismounted Confederate cavalrymen got near enough to the meeting house to see, they discovered Means' whole force standing in the yard. Fortunately, for Quaker Sam he was staying at his own house on the other side of town. As the Confederates reached the corner of the palings around the yard, Means' men seeing the advancing rebels, began to rush into the church in great confusion for safety and to return fire. Lieutenant Luther W. Slater, in charge of the men due to the absence of Captain Means, was badly wounded outside the meeting house. Various Loudoun Rangers were also wounded while entering the building escaping the onslaught. The Rangers returned fire as vigorously as circumstances would permit. Lieutenant Slater, although severely wounded, retained command until compelled by the loss of blood to relinquish that title to Drill Master Charles A. Webster.

Loudoun Ranger Lieutenant Luther W. Slater

Jack Dove and a few other Confederates sprang towards the outside windows of the meeting house. Dove fired his revolvers into the demoralized boys in blue while the others poured their buckshot through the other windows. The bullets poured through the barrier as they would through paper. The other Confederate dismounted cavalrymen dispersed to the Virts house, just opposite the meeting house and opened a violent fire.

As soon as the firing commenced White brought his cavalry down the road at a gallop and halted long enough to fire a round or two at the side windows of the meeting house. They immediately witnessed quite a few of Means' men leaping from the windows and making the fastest kind of retreat across the lot below the house and into the town. White then chased the running fellows and captured two. White also galloped down to Means' house in the hope of getting him, but he had already left. However, they did find a cache of arms at Means' residence.

Loudoun Ranger Charles A. Webster

Returning to the meeting house, White found his dismounted members laying close siege. Finally, White decided to try to negotiate surrender with the trapped Union cavalrymen. Mrs. Virts was sent under a truce, to make the proposition, but on her second mission the enemy informed her that if she came again they would shoot her. However, the drama inside the meeting house was not as confident as the message to Mrs. Virts. Loudoun Ranger John W. Forsythe believed his surrender would lead to death or imprisonment during the war.

One half of the little band had been wounded and lay around in the church pews weltering in their own blood, making the place look more like a slaughter pen than a house of worship. Then a third flag of truce was sent in. At this time the Union ammunition was entirely exhausted, and as there was no possible way of replenishing that all important article, Webster consulted Lieutenant Slater as to what was best to do under the very precarious and unfortunate circumstances. Lieutenant Slater was lying in a pew on the north side of the church, weak from the loss of blood, which was still ebbing away, his underclothes being entirely saturated, and from the wound in his right temple causing his face to be entirely covered with blood.

Loudoun Ranger Sergeant John W. Forsythe

But possessing great physical endurance, he was able to dictate a reply to Captain White's demand for a capitulation. Finally, Webster came out with a flag of truce with Lieutenant Slater's conditions. He demanded the usual terms in such cases; his men to be released on parole, their private property respected, and officers to retain their side arms; which White immediately granted and the affair was finally concluded. The Confederates gathered up fifty-six horses, saddles and bridles, about one hundred fine Union revolvers, and as many carbines, with a vast quantity of plunder, which they were unable to carry off. White paroled twenty-eight prisoners, with two previously captured, made thirty in all.

White lost Brook Hays killed and Corporal Peter J. Kabrich mortally wounded; both gallant soldiers as ever drew a saber. The enemy lost one man killed, and one who died five days later, and nine others wounded.

At the scene of surrender, when Means' men, after being formed in line, laid down their arms, it made for a curious sight. Many of them were old friends and had been schoolboys with some of White's company. In fact, in this fight, brother fought against brother; William Snoots, a sergeant in White's command, and the other, Charles Snoots, a member of Means' command, had openly fired against each other. The rebel would have most certainly have shot his Yankee brother, even after the surrender, but for the interference of one of the officers.

This would be the final episode of the fighting at the Waterford Baptist Meeting House, but part of the beginning of the war in Loudoun County.

Waterford Baptist Church

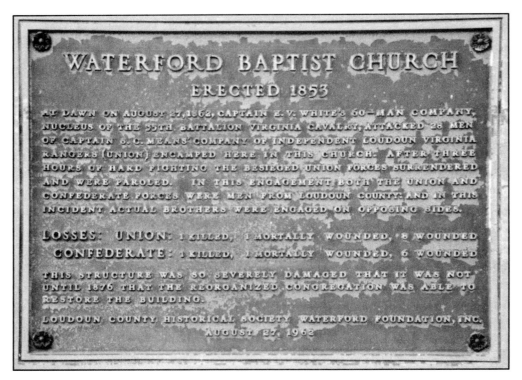

Waterford Baptist Church Marker

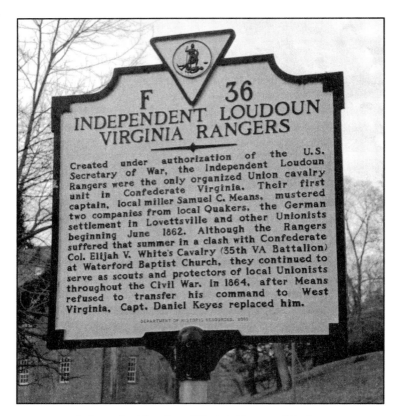

Independent Loudoun Virginia Rangers Marker

4) Samuel Means House and Mill – Mean Street and Liggett Street, Waterford

Samuel C. Means, the miller in Waterford at the start of the Civil War, was forced to flee from his home shortly after Virginia voted for secession in 1861 for refusing to raise a company for the Confederate State militia. He subsequently led the raids of the Twenty-eighth Pennsylvania Infantry Regiment under command of Colonel John W. Geary into Loudoun County, whose headquarters where located at Point of Rocks in Maryland. This caused the Confederates to offer a reward for his capture, and he was characterized as the "renegade Sam Means" and had a price put on his head. He was also known as "Quaker Sam."

Loudoun Ranger Captain Samuel "Quaker Sam" Means

Means was mustered into the United States service by Colonel Dixon S. Miles at Harper's Ferry, June 20, 1862. This was the only organized body of troops from Virginia to fight for the Union and would be known as the Independent Loudoun Virginia Rangers with Means as their Captain.

Samuel Means House (N39°11' 24" W77°36'48")

Samuel Means' Mill. The largest mill in Loudoun County. (N39°11' 24" W77°36'48")

5) Mosby fight at the Matt Lee House in December 11-15, 1862 – 41631 Olvine Place, Aldie

Matt Lee House (N38°56'45" W77°33'45")

Prior to Captain Mosby beginning his independent command, Major General J.E.B Stuart ordered Mosby to take six men to scout the Little River Turnpike in December 11-15, 1862. At Matt Lee's house, he encountered a party of Federals about equal in number to his own. Mosby and his men killed the Union sergeant in command and one private and put the others to flight.

This action only whetted Mosby's appetite for an independent command to take the fight to the enemy in Union territory as opposed to spending his time in the Confederate Army's camp.

Captain John S. Mosby

6) Mosby's receives his first nine Rangers at *Oakham* on December 29-30, 1862 – 23226 Oakham Farm Lane, Aldie (Private Property)

As J.E.B. Stuart was visiting the home of Miss Laura Ratcliffe, a staunch southern woman who lived near Frying Pan Church, in Fairfax County with Captain John Mosby on the morning of December 29, 1862, she stated to him:

"It's a shame you can't stay longer General. It's hard on us, living in conquered territory, under enemy rule."

Stuart responded:

"You are all such good Southern people through this section, I think you deserve some protection, so I shall leave Captain Mosby, with a few men, to take care of you. I want you to do all you can for him. He is a great favorite of mine and a brave soldier, and, if my judgment does not err, we shall soon hear something surprising from him."

Major General J.E.B. Stuart

Stuart was soon in the saddle again with his cavalry command on a forced march to Middleburg on the Little River Turnpike very near the Loudoun County line. Stuart was riding alone between the advance guard and the head of the column when he was joined by Mosby, who, in high spirits, was informed that at last fortune had begun to smile on him, for Stuart had promised to leave him with a detail of nine men to operate on the outposts and communication lines of the enemy.

Stuart then rode towards Colonel Hamilton Rogers' house, which was known as *Oakham*, near Dover and rested on December 29, 1862. The next day Stuart gave Mosby nine men to see what kind of damage he could do to the Union army in Fairfax, Loudoun, Prince William, and Fauquier Counties. The only man that Mosby identified as serving under him that day was his good friend Fount Beattie. No other member of the First Virginia Cavalry has been identified. The names of the other eight men is a mystery to all historians to and including the authors of this periodical.

Laura Ratcliffe

Oakham. Home of Colonel Hamilton Rogers where Mosby received his first nine Rangers (N38°58'30" W77°41'19")

Now, December 30, 1862 will forever be known as the date that John Singleton Mosby started his independent guerilla operations into Northern Virginia.

7) Mosby meets men at Mount Zion Church, heads toward Herndon on January 26 or 28, 1863 – 40309 John Mosby Highway, Aldie

Mount Zion Church (N38°57'49" W77°36'44")

In the middle of January 1863, General J.E.B. Stuart approved Mosby's request for men to conduct independent partisan operations behind enemy lines in Northern Virginia. On January 18, 1863 on a cold and rainy day Mosby and fifteen cavalrymen left the camp of the First Virginia Cavalry in King William Court House and headed towards Fauquier and Loudoun Counties. After crossing the Rappahannock at Fox's Mill, the men soon arrived at Warrenton.

As the little band marched through the town, they were stopped by the citizens, who expressed surprise when they heard that these Confederate cavalrymen had come to make war for they said Mosby's first fifteen resembled a company of missionaries, among other things, instead of a band of warriors. After leaving Warrenton the command was dispersed with orders to rendezvous on the 26th instant at Mount Zion Church, on the Little River Turnpike, a mile and a half east of Aldie. This time would not be wasted by Mosby, for while his men were searching for a place to stay plus looking for a good home to also keep their horse in the Middleburg general area, Mosby himself was occupied in collecting information. He was scouting the area learning about the position of the enemy and gaining more accurate knowledge of the country in which he would be operating.

In pursuance of orders, the command met Mosby and marched down the Little River Turnpike, but turned in the direction of Frying Pan Church where they captured a patrol of two men and then proceeded toward Old Chantilly Church where they regained the turnpike. At the church was stationed a picket of nine Union men from the Eighteenth Pennsylvania Cavalry, which Mosby determined to attack.

Covering his movements by the pines, he formed his men, and moved cautiously forward, for contrary to his former plan of attack, he decided to assail the pickets in front. Taking with him one man, Mosby dashed forward and captured the two vedettes without resistance. The command then charged the reserve, using at the same time their revolvers. The fight was a short one, and bloodless but for the wounding of one man, who was shot by Mosby when attempting to make his escape. With eleven prisoners, and their arms, horses, and equipments, the Rangers returned in high spirits to Middleburg, where as before, the prisoners were paroled and the spoil divided. The *Alexandria Gazette*, dated January 28, 1863 reported, *"On Monday night, the Confederates drove in the Federal pickets in the vicinity of Chantilly, Fairfax County."*

MOUNT ZION OLD SCHOOL BAPTIST CHURCH

Built in 1851, the Mount Zion Church was founded by conservative members of the Little River Baptist Church congregation.

During the Civil War the Church and grounds were used as a rendezvous point, barracks, prison, battlefield, hospital and burial ground.

8) Mosby attacks Colonel Sir Percy Wyndham on January 27, 1863 – 303 John Mosby Highway, Middleburg (Private Property)

Colonel Sir Percy Wyndham, a British soldier of fortune, who was born on a ship in the English Channel and had served with Garibaldi in Sicily, was the Union Brigade Cavalry Commander at Fairfax Court House in early 1863. Wyndham became so enraged by Mosby's raids into Fairfax County that he gathered two hundred men and started west on the Little River Turnpike seeking to capture Mosby and his men.

Early in the morning on January 27, 1863 as Wyndham's cavalrymen rode past Mayor Lorman Chancellor's home on the eastern entrance into Middleburg where Mosby and Fountain Beattie had been hiding and sleeping, a male slave awoke Mosby and warned them that Yankees were in the town.*

Colonel Sir Percy Wyndham

Wyndham's command had already rounded up several convalescing soldiers and old men in Middleburg. Believing that he had captured all the raiders, Wyndham started to return to his camp. Quickly, Mosby and Beattie collected seven to twelve men and attacked Wyndham's rear guard as they began to leave.

One Union trooper was killed and three captured. Wyndham, eager for a fight, wheeled his command and charged into the ensuing melee, causing Fount Beattie's horse to slip on the icy road and fall. Beattie, Thomas Beaty, and Edward Walters were all captured and were taken to Old Capitol Prison but were soon exchanged. Mosby was riding a fast horse and was able to escape. Mosby would watch the Union cavalrymen leaving from the street daring them to fire at him. Mosby would later ride to a nearby hill outside Middleburg suitable for watching the Union troops as they headed back to Fairfax.

Mosby Ranger Fount Beattie

Wyndham claimed that he captured twenty-four of Mosby's men that morning. Mosby wrote, *"Colonel Sir Percy Wyndham, with over two hundred cavalry, came up to Middleburg last week to punish me…I had a slight skirmish with him, in which my loss was three men, captured by the falling of their horses…Fount Beattie was one of the Rangers captured."*

303 John Mosby Highway, Middleburg (N38°58'12" W77°43'53")

* Others claim that Mosby and Beattie were hiding in the house next to or east of Lorman Chancellor's house as Wyndham rode into Middleburg. That house is the yellow house at 303 John Mosby Highway. Lorman Chancellor's house is located at 301 John Mosby Highway and is pictured in the story about Mosby staying at Lorman Chancellor's house before the Fairfax Courthouse raid.

9) Mosby visits Matt Lee House between February 2-4, 1863 – 41631 Olvine Place, Aldie

Mosby visited the Matt Lee house for supper before traveling to Frying Pan in Fairfax County and halted between February 2nd and 4th at Ben Hatton's house, a Yankee sympathizer. Mosby forced Hatton to lead him to the location of the local Union picket post of the Eighteenth Pennsylvania Cavalry by threatening to send Hatton to prison in Richmond.

Mosby's attack on the post was swift, and he captured eleven prisoners whose plan had been to lure Mosby in and capture him. Mosby's report read: *"The Federals set a nice trap to catch me, but contrary to their expectations; I brought the trap off with me."*

10) Mosby asked to stop his guerilla operation by the citizens of Middleburg on February 2-4, 1863 – Red Fox Inn, 2 East Washington Street, Middleburg

Colonel Sir Percy Wyndham continued to become agitated by Mosby's unforeseen escapades and raids upon his outposts, pickets, and scouting parties in, along, and near the Little River Turnpike during the entire month of January 1863 as Mosby started his guerilla operations. Knowing that Mosby and his men were staying in Middleburg and were basing their operations from that illustrious little village, Wyndham repeatedly threatened to burn the town of Middleburg and ravage the countryside between it and Fairfax Court House. Finally, the good citizens took a petition to Mosby, requesting him to withdraw from their midst.

Mosby replied in writing to Mayor Lorman A. Chancellor and citizens Francis W. Powell, I. G. Gray, and William Burr Noland:

> *I have just received your petition requesting me to discontinue my warfare on the Yankees, because they have threatened to burn your town and destroy your property in retaliation for my acts. Not being prepared for any such degrading compromise with the Yankees, I unhesitatingly refuse to comply. My attacks on scouts, patrols, and pickets, which have provoked this threat, are sanctioned both by the custom of war and the practice of the enemy, and you are at liberty to inform them that no such clamor shall deter me from employing whatever legitimate weapon I can most efficiently use for their annoyance.*

Mosby refused to leave Middleburg, and Wyndham never burned down the town. Threats did not work when dealing with the Gray Ghost.

11) Six Rangers caught dancing on February 6, 1863 – Aldie

A detachment from Companies H & F, Fifth New York Cavalry, commanded by Union Captain James Penfield, made a raid into Middleburg and at Aldie captured six members of Mosby's gang and the Postmaster of Little Washington. The Rangers were attending a ball in violation of Mosby's orders given to them by the citizens of Aldie at the McCarty's place. Four of the Rangers captured were Charles Buchanan, George McClarey, Jack Morgan, and Edward Williams. They were excellently mounted and their horses were also captured.

Aldie, Virginia

12) Ball's Mill on February 7, 1863 – 21766 Evergreen Mills Road, Leesburg

Mill Stones from Ball's Mill (N39°01'14" W77°34'34")

On February 7, 1863, the Rangers were ordered to assemble at Ball's Mill on Goose Creek not far from the Loudoun and Fairfax line. But only five of the men appeared at the rendezvous, six of them having been captured by Union raiders the night before at a dancing party which they had attended in violation of Mosby's orders.

It was the purpose of Mosby to have renewed an attack on the picket-line in Fairfax, but hearing of a Union foraging party was in the neighborhood, he resolved to follow them. The Union plunderers, who were acting more like robbers rather than soldiers, had not only taken with them the horses of citizens, which in war are regarded as contraband, but had also stripped clean all the valuables which they could carry off including silver spoons, jewelry, and the clothing of ladies from the various dwelling-houses situated in their line of march.

While chasing these marauders, Mosby ran into an old country doctor, Dr. Francis Drake walking home through the knee deep mud and snow. Dr. Drake informed Mosby that he had been making his rounds, visiting his patients, when he had met a body of Union cavalry in the road. They had robbed Dr. Drake of his horse, saddlebags, and all of his medicines.

As medicine was extremely scarce in the Confederacy, medicine was more valuable than gold so this was a severe loss to the community even by the loss of Dr. Drake's small stock. Dr. Drake told Mosby that outlaws were not far ahead, so Mosby spurred on to overtake them. When the Union thieves had reached a point within a few miles of Dranesville, Mosby and his Rangers soon over took the party of seven, which had halted to examine their booty. Mosby easily caught up with this Union raiding party because they were more intent on saving themselves and their plunder than in fighting. When the robbers saw Mosby, they scampered away with the Rangers close behind them.

Very soon Mosby came to a narrow stream, the Horsepen Run, which was booming from the melting snows. The foremost Union man on the fleetest horse, who was some distance in front of the others, plunged in and narrowly escaped being drowned. He got a good dunking and was glad to become a prisoner. His companions did not try to swim after him but preferred to quietly submit to manifest destiny instead. They were loaded with their silver spoons and valuables they had taken, but the chief prize was old Doctor Drake's saddlebags, which they had not opened.

The silver was returned to the owners and the prisoners were sent to Richmond. One can only imagine how Dr. Drake felt when his medicine and surgical implements were returned to his stead.

13) Mosby attacks Union Major Joseph Gilmore on March 2, 1863 at Aldie Mill – 39401 John Mosby Highway, Aldie

Aldie Mill (N38°58'31" W77°38'29")

Early in the morning hours of March 2, 1863, Union Major Joseph Gilmore with about two hundred troopers from the Eighteenth Pennsylvania Cavalry and the Fifth New York Cavalry surrounded and entered the town of Middleburg and slowly searched each house for Mosby's Rangers. The Union soldiers found no enemy cavalrymen but gathered a number of elderly men and old cripples on crutches out of bed. Gilmore ordered the prisoners to be formed in the street and they were forced to march in place to stay warm in the frigid air. During the ransacking of Middleburg, the Union cavalrymen discovered various barrels of liquor which were gladly consumed. Major Gilmore also actively engaged in the tasting of the various stimulants.

When Mosby and seventeen Rangers arrived in Middleburg after Gilmore left, they were met by a number of women grieving over the capture of their dear husbands and loved ones. Mosby immediately left the town to follow Gilmore's path.

As Mosby was galloping down Little River Turnpike, while ascending a hill on the outskirts of Aldie, Mosby captured two Union cavalrymen who came out to meet them by mistake. Mosby later wrote, *"Neither party had been aware of the approach of the other, and our meeting was so unexpected that our horses' heads nearly butted together before we could stop."*

After taking them prisoner Mosby charged into the hamlet full speed while riding a high-spirited untested horse, which became completely unmanageable. Scattered about and lying around the Aldie Mill was a considerable body of dismounted Union troopers with their horses hitched to fence posts while feeding at the mill. Seeing the Confederates riding toward them, the Union troopers ran and dispersed in every direction.

As Mosby raced into Aldie, he quickly lost control of his spirited steed, an animal described by Mosby as *"a splendid horse – a noble bay – who had got his mettle up,"* and headed pell-mell through the Union troops. Mosby saved himself by leaping from the saddle as his startled mount reached the narrow bridge just past the Mill over the Little River exiting the village. Ranger Henry Furlong Carter quickly dismounted and offered his horse to Mosby to rejoin the combat.

Aldie Bridge where Mosby leaped from his mount. 39459 John Mosby Highway (N38°58'30" W77°38'21")

It turned out it was not Gilmore's men that Mosby had attacked, but Companies H & M of the First Vermont Cavalry returning from an early morning scouting expedition at Dranesville. Captain Franklin T. Huntoon, Company H, had led a patrol of fifty-nine men and had stopped to rest in Aldie. Some of the Vermonters had dismounted and were lounging about the Mill until they were surprised by Mosby.

During the attack, several troopers tried to escape and hide by burrowing into the flour inside the gristmill. The Rangers enjoyed digging out the hiding Vermonters with their uniforms completely covered in white flour. The Confederates took nineteen prisoners including Captains Huntoon and John W. Woodward, Company M, and twenty-three horses. Legend had it that Mosby captured nineteen ghosts that day.

During the fight, Union Captain Woodward's horse was killed pinning him to the ground. Ranger William Thomas "Tom" Turner from Prince George's County, Maryland, rode up and demanded the captain's surrender. Woodward drew a pocket revolver from his coat which contained two shots and fired, slightly wounding Turner. Turner was irate and claimed that the Union captain had shot him after surrendering. Woodward stated that he had shot Turner in a fair fight. Mosby would leave the severely injured Woodward with a family in Aldie to care for him, as he was too severely wounded to be moved. However, Woodward would recover but not survive the war. He would be killed on July 6, 1863, near Hagerstown, Maryland during the Gettysburg campaign.

Lieutenant Colonel Robert Johnstone stated, *"Fifty men of the First Vermont Cavalry, from Companies H and M, under Captains Huntoon and Woodward were surprised in Aldie while feeding their horses by about seventy of the enemy...Major Gilmore has returned....and saw but one rebel."*

As for Gilmore, he had seen troopers and believed them to be the Confederates who were trying to trap and capture him. Gilmore immediately left the Little River Turnpike and took the Braddock Road back to his camp in Centerville. Unbeknownst to him, the patrol he was fleeing was the First Vermont Cavalry. When Gilmore's men heard the gunfire in Aldie, they truly believed that Mosby was after them. Mosby with a handful of men scared Gilmore and his two hundred men so convincingly that they abandoned their prisoners and rode so hard for over ten long miles that they completely exhausted and almost ruined their mounts. It was a most disgraceful display of Union leadership.

Subsequently, a military tribunal was ordered and charges were brought against Gilmore for drunkenness and cowardice. He was court-martialed on Friday, March 27, 1863, and found guilty of the charge of drunkenness, but not guilty of cowardice. However, Gilmore was sentenced to be cashiered out of the Union Army. Mosby had ruined Gilmore's career in the U.S. Cavalry.

14) Mosby at Lorman Chancellor House on March 8, 1863 – 301 John Mosby Highway, Middleburg (Private Property)

Lorman Chancellor House (N38°58'12" W77°43'53")

The stone house on the east end of Middleburg was the residence of Mosby's good friend, Lorman Chancellor, the mayor of Middleburg and a Colonel of the militia. It was at this house that Mosby ate dinner before he left to meet his men at Dover for the raid into Fairfax Court House on March 8, 1863 where he captured Union Brigadier General Edwin Stoughton. It was while leaving the mayor's house where Mosby wrote in his memoirs the following statement:

"I shall mount the stars tonight or sink lower than plummet ever sounded."

Captain John S. Mosby

30

15) Mosby stops at Ball's Mill and Nat Skinner's house on March 16, 1863 – 40513 John Mosby Highway, Aldie (Private Property)

On the 16th of March 1863, Mosby notified his men to meet at Rector's Crossroads in Fauquier County. In response to his call, forty men assembled. The command was drawn up, and General Stuart's order in reference to the capture of Union Brigadier General Edwin Stoughton was read and was received with a round of cheers.

Headquarters Cavalry Division,
March 12, 1863.

General Orders.

    Captain John S. Mosby has for a long time attracted the attention of his generals by his boldness, skill, and success, so signally displayed in his numerous forays upon the invaders of his native soil. None know his daring enterprise and dashing heroism better than those foul invaders, those strangers themselves to such noble traits.

    His last brilliant exploit - the capture of Brigadier-General Stoughton, U. S. A., two captains, and thirty other prisoners, together with their arms, equipments, and fifty-eight horses - justifies this recognition in General Orders. This feat, almost unparalleled in the war, was performed in the midst of the enemy's troops, at Fairfax Court House, without loss or injury.

    The gallant band of Captain Mosby shares the glory, as they did the danger of this enterprise, and are worthy of such a leader.

J. E. B. Stuart,
Major-General Commanding.

Nat Skinner House (N38°57'41" W77°36'07")

They then proceeded down the Little River Turnpike until they reached a point below Middleburg, where they struck across the country to their left until they reached the neighborhood of Ball's Mill. Here the men were divided into two parties, one of which was sent with Dick Moran to find quarters at the house of a citizen, while Mosby, with the other party, passed the night with Mosby's friend Nat Skinner.

At an early hour the next day, the command was brought together and marched in the direction of Dranesville. Only John Underwood was told by Mosby where they were going.

16) Mosby surprised by the First Vermont Cavalry at Miskell's Farm on March 31, 1863 – April 1, 1863 – 20082 Dairy Lane, Sterling (Private Property)

Miskell's Farm House (N39°3'37" W77°25'55")

On March 31, 1863, Mosby called a gathering of his men in Rector's Crossroads. Mosby with sixty-nine men departed for Dranesville expecting to find a large Union cavalry party in that locale and do battle. Not finding the enemy in the area, the disappointed unit headed west on the turnpike towards Leesburg. As the command marched from Dranesville, Dick Moran, who came from that neighborhood, stopped to pass the night with an old acquaintance Mr. Henry Green, who lived on the road about midway between Dranesville and Miskell's.

At around ten o'clock at night, Mosby decided to spend the night at Miskell's Farm, which is about a half mile from the pike where Mosby and his men had ridden that night. Dense woodland extended halfway between the turnpike on both sides of the road towards Miskell's, which was situated on the summit of a hill. At the northern base, a half a mile in the distance, flowed the Potomac.

The barn-yard and farmhouse, in which the command was encamped, was surrounded by a high white picket fence with a high narrow plantation gate that was situated two hundred yards from the barn. When the Rangers arrived at the farmhouse, Mosby could plainly see the campfires of a Union signal station on the opposite side of the river. The majority of Mosby's men took refuge in the barn. Mosby and a few other Rangers slept in the kitchen near the fireplace inside the Miskell home.

Unfortunately, due to the inclement weather, it being late at night, and everyone being tired from the hard days ride, Mosby did not post any sentinels before going to sleep.

Fireplace at Miskell's Farmhouse where Mosby slept before the fight

At two o'clock on the morning on April 1, 1863, while Mosby was asleep, Captain Henry Flint and one hundred and fifty men belonging to the First Vermont Cavalry were on the move seeking Mosby's Conglomerates as they were initially called at that time. As the confident officer moved off, he exclaimed, *"All right, boys; we will give Mosby an April fool!"* Flint's men responded with a loud cheer. Unfortunately, the Vermonters would ride some six hours in the cold over muddy roads and were wearing heavy overcoats before they would encounter and engage the Rangers later that morning.

Union Captain Henry Flint

About daylight, Flint and the First Vermont Cavalry passed the home of Henry Green where Moran was staying and stopped there for information. Moran hid until Flint rode off and then speedily mounted his horse, and took a short cut across the intervening farmland to warn Mosby of their impending danger.

Mr. Henry Green's House

Mosby arose at sunrise and noticed the Signal Station across the Potomac was very active and he wondered what was going on so early in the morning. At that moment, Dick Moran came riding across the field shouting, *"Mount up boys! The Yankees are coming!"* In just a few seconds the camp came alive with excitement and the men hurried to grab their arms and saddle their horses.

The Vermont cavalry had already passed through a narrow gate and were starting to encircle the farmhouse and form in line of battle almost one hundred yards away. The last Union troopers had closed the gate so none of the Confederates could launch their escape. Flint called out to his men to *"shoot the d---d cowards."* The Vermonters first volley however was ineffective.

Mosby noticed that his men were already mounted, and he opened the barnyard gate waving and shouting his men forward to attack. Mosby at once called out to his men to rally and told them they had to fight! Mosby's horse was unsaddled, so Mosby then pulled out his revolvers and started running towards the First Vermont Cavalry firing as he ran.

Ranger Harry Hatcher seeing his leader on foot dismounted said, *"Captain, take my horse"* and gallantly gave his mount to his revered commander. Anywhere from twenty to thirty Rangers were racing towards the First Vermont boys with their revolvers raging violence with each shot. Hatcher, mounting a Yankee horse, whose rider had been shot, soon followed in the attack. Captain Flint was the first to fall with half a dozen bullets lodged in his body.

Mosby Ranger Harry Hatcher

The Union troopers froze in surprise seeing Flint fall in the front, and the Rangers heading straight towards them firing their pistols, yelling and screaming. Both sides were soon engaged in hand to hand fighting. The Union assailants soon began to flee and retreat until they noticed that they were the ones now trapped by the closed narrow gateway. Here, the slaughter of the First Vermonters was the greatest as a crowd of Mosby's men emptied their pistols into the jammed mass of Vermonters. Finally, the gate barrier gave way, and the frightened and disorderly Union troopers scattered through the opening to the woods outside the fence and along the road leading to the turnpike, hotly pursued by the defiant Rangers.

Dick Moran overtook a Vermont trooper in the woods and demanded his surrender. But the Vermonter was made of better stuff and being an accomplished swordsman closed with Moran, who certainly would have been killed or injured in this encounter if it was not for Harry Hatcher coming to his relief firing a round from his pistol terminating the conflict.

The Reverend Sam Chapman, who had already exhausted every barrel of his two pistols, drew his trusty saber and was among the foremost of the pursuers. Sam having already killed two Vermonters, as he dashed among two others, demanded their surrender. Unfortunately for Chapman, he met with the same fate as Moran with the two Union foes vigorously attacking him, with one of them giving Chapman a severe saber cut on the head. The reverend was now in a very serious predicament until

Mosby Ranger William Hunter

William Hunter rode up forcing both of the Yankees to raise their arms in surrender.

Mosby Ranger Captain William Chapman

The Rangers chased the fleeing Vermonters all the way to Dranesville and two miles beyond. George Whitescarver, George Siebert, Welt Hatcher, John Wild, Harry Hatcher, and the Reverend Sam Chapman were all identified following the fleeing Yankees. William Chapman was captured by one of the Vermonters, but one of the Rangers came to his rescue and set him free. Prior to that, Chapman had fired six shots and emptied five Union saddles. However, Mosby praised William's brother Samuel for his bravery during the fight and promoted him to Captain after the affair.

Mosby Ranger Ned Hurst

Mosby suffered one Ranger mortally wounded, Davis of Kentucky, whose first name was never recorded, and three wounded; Edward "Ned" Hurst of Fauquier County, Robert Hart of the Black Horse Troop, and William Keys.

Robert Hart, Black Horse Troop

Mosby killed 9 Union cavalrymen, captured 82 prisoners, and 95 excellent horses. Lieutenant Charles A. Woodbury, Company B, attempted to rally his men, but was killed by a pistol shot to the head from James F. "Big Yankee" Ames.

Believed to be Mosby Ranger "Big Yankee" Ames in Union uniform

Union Lieutenant Josiah Grout

Lieutenant Josiah Grout was thought to be seriously wounded and was left to die at Miskell's Farm but recovered to become governor of Vermont and to meet and talk with Mosby after the war. The bullet that entered Grout's body was still lodged in his right leg when he met with the former guerilla chieftain.

Union Captain George H. Bean never took part in the fight but was the first to skedaddle twelve miles and reach camp. When he rode in bareheaded, shouting, *"The Rebels are upon us!"*…Bean would be dismissed from the service for his cowardly conduct that morning at Miskell's Farm. I guess the April Fool's joke was on him!

Miskell Farm Plaque

Fight at Miskell's Farm. Courtesy of William Anderson descendent of Joe Nelson

Fight at Miskell Farm. Courtesy of Arthur DeButts. Depicted at left-center is John S. Mosby; to his right is Harry Hatcher, and to Hatcher's right is George Slater; Ed Hurst is peering over Mosby's left shoulder; to Mosby's left is Joseph Nelson, and behind Nelson is John deButts; at right is Samuel Chapman with sabre raised: in front of Mosby is the mortally wounded Captain Henry Flint of the First Vermont.

39

17) Broad Run Toll House and Bridge – Route 7 and Route 28 Intersection, Sterling

Broad Run Toll House along the old Leesburg and Alexandria Turnpike (N39°2'49" W77°25'58")

Remains of Broad Run Toll Bridge along the old Leesburg and Alexandria Turnpike

The Broad Run tollhouse was built about 1820 and still stands adjacent to a double-arch stone bridge. The old tollhouse was also known as the Broad Run Post Office for that vicinity from 1854 to 1869.

The Leesburg and Alexandria turnpike was built by the various farmers and millers in the area who needed good roads to move their produce or goods to Alexandria. The toll to Leesburg by wagon, or horse was 50 cents. Mosby and his Rangers passed this house many times during the war.

18) Approximate location of Mr. Henry Green's House – Davenport Drive and Route 7, Sterling

Approximate location of Henry Green House (N39°2'8" W77°24'38")

Dick Moran stopped here for information the night before the fight at Miskell Farm. Captain Henry Flint and the First Vermont Cavalry passed the farm on the morning of the fight. Moran hid until the Union soldiers had passed before riding furiously to warn Mosby yelling, *"The Yankees are coming!"* giving Mosby just enough time to prepare for the Union attack.

19) Union cavalry capture three Rangers on April 27, 1863 – Aldie

At daybreak on April 27th, 1863, Union commander General Julius Stahel of the Cavalry division in Fairfax, charged with defending the city of Washington, took two of his best brigades, numbering 2,500 men and a battery of four guns on a scout along the Little River Turnpike for the purpose of finding and wiping out Mosby and his entire command. During the march at Aldie, the Federals only captured three Rangers; Thomas Green, Lycurgus Hutchison, and one other only identified as Thompson in addition to seven citizens who were not Rangers. An unsatisfactory affair at best.

Union General Julius Stahel

Mosby Ranger Lycurgus Hutchison (c1914)

20) Fight at Blakely's Grove on May 6, 1863 – Greengarden and Millville Roads, Upperville

On May 6, 1863, Major Mosby and Rangers Edwin Rowzee and James J. Williamson were at the house of George S. Ayre near Upperville having dinner. When dinner was over, their host came into the room and said, *"The Yankees are coming!"* Mosby picked up his hat and pistols, mounted his horse, which stood ready and rode off.

Rowzee and Williamson started to the stable to get their horses, but before they reached it, heard firing in the woods at Blakely's Grove about a mile from the house. They halted and in a few moments saw a blue-coat skirmish line on the crest of a hill opposite, and soon a body of infantry came into view. They concealed themselves behind a stone fence and crept along watching them as they moved towards Upperville.

Mosby Ranger James Williamson

A farm bell which was used to call the hands from the fields to the house was sounded at this time, and the Federal infantry, evidently thinking it a signal, halted and drew up in line. Rowzee and Williamson hastened back to the house where they were told there had been a fight in the woods and a number of wounded men were there. They threw off their coats and jumped into an ox-cart which stood nearby and with a Negro driver hurried off to the scene of the fight.

As they neared the place a Union cavalryman rode up and said: *"Are there any rebels in the neighborhood? "I don't know,"* said Williamson. The Union cavalryman said they had been attacked by about one hundred and fifty rebels. In the woods they found five wounded, and in the road one man and two horses killed. The main body had gone towards Upperville, while a few had been left to look after the wounded who were taken temporarily to the school house at the grove.

Blakely's Grove. Corner of Greengarden and Millville Roads (N39°01'0" W77°51'13")

One of the Union privates was very communicative. He told Williamson they had two killed and six wounded; that among the wounded was Lieutenants William H. Boyd and Jesse F. Wyckoff of the First New York Cavalry, and Lieutenant Henry J. Hawkins of the Sixth Maryland Cavalry. About twenty cavalrymen from the First New York Cavalry had ridden toward Upperville on the Bloomfield Road. The Sixty-seventh Pennsylvania Infantry remained near Blakely's Grove, a farm north of Upperville to set up an ambuscade.

The Union leadership was attempting to lure Mosby into an infantry ambush and use Mosby's tactics against him. Near Blakely's Grove, between Bloomfield and Upperville, fifteen of Mosby's men charged the Union cavalry. The Union troopers started running back towards their own infantry, but they were greeted with an unwelcome volley of musketry. Unfortunately, the Pennsylvanians were so excited they did not wait for the Confederates to come up and fired on their own men. Only one Ranger, Robert Gray was slightly wounded. The Rangers instinctively discovered the trap and quickly wheeled their horses however and were soon out of range.

Ranger Charles Buchanan was also seriously wounded and was taken to the home of Hal and Ida Dulany, situated off the road about a mile east of Upperville. Jacob Fisher, a private in Company I, First Virginia Cavalry, was captured the next day near Snickersville by the Sixty-seventh Pennsylvania. He claimed he was on detached duty with Mosby's command. Fisher, who was from New Orleans, remained in prison until he joined the First U.S. Volunteers on February 27, 1864 at Point Lookout, Maryland. He then deserted the Union Army at Camp Reno, Milwaukee, Wisconsin on September 14, 1864 and finally made his way back South and returned to duty with the First Virginia Cavalry sometime around December 1864.

21) ***The Maples*, Home of Mosby Ranger Robert W. Fletcher and site of an incident on May 13, 1863 – Route 50 and Rokeby Road, Upperville (Private Property)**

The Maples. **Home of Mosby Ranger Robert Fletcher (N38°59′19″ W77°50′30″)**

As early as 1786, *The Maples* was the home of Isaac Gibson, who came with his mother's family from Pennsylvania about twenty years before and settled in the Upperville neighborhood. The next owner of the property was James Bowles who married Elizabeth Gibson in February 1803. Before the War Between the States, *The Maples* belonged to Joshua Fletcher who had a large family of sons and daughters, all of whom became highly respected and active citizens of the community. At least three of his sons served in the Confederate Army. It is rumored that Joshua Fletcher dropped dead literally "on the spot" when during a Civil War skirmish nearby *The Maples* when an errant shell came through the dining room window, leaving its mark on a dining room door, still evident.

On May 13, 1863, Captain William H. Boyd with one hundred troopers belonging to the First New York Cavalry rode towards Upperville and encountered fifty of Mosby's Rangers and chased them several miles attempting to kill or capture them. One of the troopers of the First New York Cavalry, Patrick Donnelly was left at Mr. Fletcher's house. Donnelly was well cared for and the Fletcher family even obtained medicine for him. According to Donnelly, Mosby himself called several times to see him and treated him with the greatest kindness. After the war, Donnelly made his home in the Upperville area.

One son, Robert W. Fletcher, was the Commissary sergeant in the Seventh Virginia Cavalry and had previously served in Captain Welby Carter's Company A, First Virginia Cavalry having his right arm nearly shot off at First Manassas on July 21, 1861. On August 15, 1863, Fletcher was "arrested on the banks of Rappahannock with four horses which he intended to sell to rebels." Later Captain Walter Frankland enlisted Fletcher for the rest of the war into the Forty-third Battalion Virginia Cavalry on September 7, 1864. He was "returned to the infantry on October 17, 1864 by order of Colonel Mosby."

Another son, Captain John W. Fletcher, who had gone to the Virginia Military Institute and had joined the Seventh Virginia Cavalry, was killed while fighting at Buckton Station on May 23, 1862. This is how he died:

Early that morning of May 13, 1863, Confederate Colonel Turner Ashby formed his cavalry in line and charged the train station but was driven back by one hundred and forty Union Wisconsin infantrymen. Ordering another charge, Ashby's cavalry forced the Union infantrymen to finally give way and leave the depot. The Union infantry fell back across the field and set up a new defensive line in a railroad embankment. Ashby's men hurriedly set fire to the station and severed the telegraph line. Colonel Ashby then ordered his column to charge the new Union line of defense. Unfortunately, the Confederate cavalry dashed forward recklessly over fences, rough ground, rode into every other intervening obstacle, and were driven back losing two of their most trusted officers. In that charge Ashby lost twenty-seven year old Captain John Fletcher. Fletcher was wounded in the arm and his horse carried him into the enemy lines where he was again shot and killed. Major General Thomas Jonathan "Stonewall" Jackson called Captain Fletcher, *"one of the most valuable officers with his cavalry."*

John's other brother Clinton Fletcher, who also served in the Seventh Virginia Cavalry, had his horse shot out from under him at Buckton Station, Virginia and was mortally wounded at Greenland Gap, West Virginia on April 25, 1863 dying the very next day.

All three brothers are buried in Ivy Hill Cemetery in Upperville, Fauquier County, Virginia. In the east wall of the house is a hole made by a Union cannon shot in the fighting between General J.E.B. Stuart's cavalry and General Alfred Pleasanton's cavalry.

22) Rangers captured on June 12, 1863 – Middleburg

On June 11, 1863, Union Major John Hammond of the Fifth New York Cavalry was ordered to march with a large number of men west along the Little River Turnpike in an attempt to intercept Mosby's men returning from a raid at Seneca Mills in Maryland. When Hammond arrived in Middleburg, he found that Mosby had already arrived, disbanded his Ranger, and disappeared into the countryside.

Union Major John Hammond, Fifth New York Cavalry

When the New Yorkers searched the village, they found a few Rangers hiding in some of the houses. Captain James William Foster, recently elected the first captain of Company A on June 10, 1863; George Turberville; Minor Lee Thompson; the notorious Charles McDonough; and the famous scout and spy Frank Stringfellow were among those captured near or in the town. They were later released and rejoined Mosby's Command.

Mosby Ranger James Foster

Mosby Ranger George Turberville

46

Mosby Ranger Minor Lee Thompson

Confederate Scout and Spy Frank Stringfellow

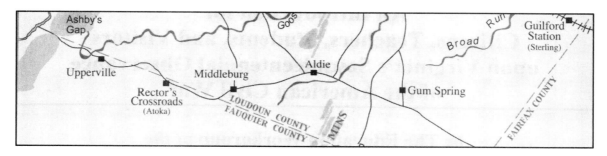

Middleburg, Virginia

23) General J.E.B. Stuart met Major Mosby and his men in front of the Red Fox Inn on June 17, 1863 – 2 East Washington Street, Middleburg

Red Fox Inn (N39°58′8″ W77°44′7″)

Colonel John S. Mosby

Late in the afternoon of June 17, 1863, Major Mosby rode into Middleburg with thirty-five or forty Rangers. Mosby found Stuart surrounded by quite a few very young ladies in the street in front of the Red Fox Inn. Stuart made some jocular remarks about Mosby's men as they passed.

Stuart and Mosby held a short conference and Stuart approved of the expedition where Mosby was intending to cross the Potomac and attack the Union camps

Major General J.E.B. Stuart

around Seneca Mills, Maryland. Mosby bade Stuart good bye and told him he would soon hear from him and subsequently headed out of town striking towards the Potomac.

24) James Gulick's home, June 17, 1863. National Beagle Club – 22265 Oatlands Road, Aldie

Farmer James Gulick's House (N39°0′28″ W77°39′37″)

On June 17, 1863, after the short meeting with General J.E.B. Stuart at the Red Fox Inn in Middleburg, the Confederate Partisan chieftain John Singleton Mosby with thirty or forty Rangers headed towards the Potomac. Mosby's plan was to attack the Union camps situated at Seneca Mills, Maryland.

While enroute, Mosby rode on the Snickersville Turnpike and stopped at the house of a farmer named James Franklin Gulick for a while to rest and refresh himself with buttermilk on a hot day under the shade of some trees. Gulick purchased the Loudoun Agricultural and Mechanical Institute on the grounds of *Oak Hill* in 1846 for only $4,821, and he was living there during the Civil War.

While there, Mosby and his men heard artillery firing over towards Aldie which indicated an engagement of the enemy's cavalry with Stuart's. Mosby and every one of his men mounted immediately. From a commanding position on the mountain which Mosby reached in a few minutes, he could see clouds of dust rising on every road which showed that Union General Fighting Joe Hooker was marching for the Potomac while Union General Alfred Pleasanton's Cavalry was fighting in Aldie.

Due to the large number of Union cavalry in the area, Mosby decided not to proceed to Seneca Mills as planned and proceeded to scout the surrounding area of the battle around Aldie to attempt to capture some "prizes" and assist Stuart if he could.

25) Mosby captures Major Sterling and Captain Fisher at the Almond Birch House on June 17, 1863 – 24217 Goshen Road and John Mosby Highway, Aldie

Location of Almond Birch House (N38°56'48" W77°33'54")

At ten o'clock on Thursday night, June 17, 1863, hours after leaving James Gulick's house, Mosby accompanied by Joe Nelson, Norman Smith, and Charles L. Hall, penetrated the Federal lines east of Aldie. While on the Little River Turnpike the four Rangers saw a Union column and rode confidently right into their ranks and joined them on their march as they passed along. As it was dark, the Union troopers had no suspicion who they were, although they were all dressed in full Confederate uniform.

Mosby Ranger Joe Nelson

Mosby Ranger Norman Smith

Mosby Ranger Sergeant Charles Landon Hall

Union Captain Benjamin F. Fisher

Outside of Aldie at the Almond Birch House, Mosby captured two Federal officers and an orderly. One of the officers was Captain Benjamin F. Fisher, a signal officer, and the other, Major William R. Sterling, the bearer of important dispatches from Hooker to Pleasanton.

When Mosby and his entourage arrived at the Almond Birch place at ten o'clock, they noticed three horses standing at Birch's front gate with a man holding them by their bridles. Mosby rode up and asked him to whom they belonged. The Union soldier replied that they were Major Sterling's and Captain Fisher's, and that they were just from General Hooker's headquarters. Mosby called the horse holder up to him and took him by the collar and leaning down whispered in his ear: *"You are my prisoner. My name is Mosby."* The man, who was an Irishman, recognized the name Mosby and indignantly replied, *"You are a d—d liar. I am as good a Union man as you are."* Just then in the starlight he saw the gleam of Mosby's pistol and had nothing further to say.

In a few minutes, the officers came out of the house. Mosby saluted them and asked which way they were going and where they were from. As Mosby seemed to be in such friendly relations with their orderly, they never suspected who they were talking to and promptly answered that they were from General Hooker's headquarters and were carrying dispatches to Pleasanton.

51

Captain Fisher was his chief signal officer, going up to establish a signal station at Snicker's gap—if he could get there.

By this time, Mosby's comrades dismounted. As Mosby was talking to Major Sterling, Joe Nelson walked up politely extended his hand and asked for his pistol. Charlie Hall, not to be outdone in courtesy by Nelson, proposed to relieve Captain Fisher of his arms. They both misunderstood what Hall and Nelson meant and offered to shake hands with them.

In an instant, the barrels of four glittering revolvers informed them that death was their doom if they refused to be prisoners. Resistance was useless, and they all surrendered. All now mounted quickly and rode off and left the pike. As they started, both officers burst out laughing. Mosby asked them what they were laughing at. They said they had laughed so much about their people being gobbled up by Mosby that they were now enjoying the joke being turned on themselves.

Mosby went to a nearby farmer's house, got a light, and read the dispatches. Mosby then sent Nelson and Hall off with the prisoners and sent Smith with the dispatches to report to Stuart. After being exchanged, Captain Fisher would later become a Union brigadier general on March 13, 1865.

26) Battle of Aldie Memorial at the Furr House, June 17, 1863 – 40590 Snickersville Turnpike, Aldie (Private Property). First Massachusetts Cavalry Marker – Snickersville Turnpike near New Oatlands Road

Furr House (N38°59'30" W77°39'50")

A piece of ground, ten feet square, marking the location of where one hundred and ninety-six troopers of the First Massachusetts Cavalry were wounded or killed in action during the fighting of Aldie on June 17, 1863, was generously donated after the war by Dallas Furr for the site of a special Union monument. Furr, who was formerly a Confederate Ranger in Mosby's command and whose family and house were located nearby, kindly treated and cared for the wounded Union cavalrymen after the fighting. The survivors of the First Massachusetts Cavalry sent a fine Morris gold mounted chair as a testimonial to Dallas Furr and his family for their generosity.

A beautiful monument was erected on the property to commemorate the "Battle of the Haystacks," on June 17, 1863, in which the First Massachusetts Cavalry played such a significant role.

First Massachusetts Cavalry Monument, Snickersville Turnpike near New Oatlands Road (N39°13'23" W77°34'35")

53

27) Mount Defiance. Site of Fighting between Aldie and Middleburg on June 19, 1863 – 36001 John Mosby Highway between Aldie and Middleburg

On June 19, 1863, the Ninth Virginia Cavalry and the Thirteenth Virginia Cavalry were driven from Mount Defiance by the Tenth New York Cavalry. Mosby and his men would have ridden by this location many times during the war.

Mount Defiance (N38°58′4″ W77°45′42″)

28) Death of the New York Herald Correspondent on June 22, 1863 – 40309 John Mosby Highway, Mount Zion Church, Aldie

Lynde Walter Buckingham was killed on June 22nd, 1863, while serving as a correspondent for the *New York Herald*. Buckingham had spent the day of June 21, 1863 covering what would become one of the most interesting cavalry battles of the war in and around Aldie, Middleburg, and Upperville.

After the June 21, 1863 engagement around Upperville, Buckingham was on his way to Washington City with his account of the fighting when Confederate Partisan fighters under Mosby's command overtook him causing his horse to dash down a steep hill and throwing Buckingham forcefully to the ground cracking his skull. Buckingham was treated in a makeshift

54

Union Army hospital and later died of head injuries and was buried within the Mount Zion Church cemetery.

Wounded Union soldiers were cared for inside Mount Zion Church from July 17-21, 1863

Alfred R. Waud, the renowned Civil War artist for *Harpers Ferry Weekly* dug the grave for his friend. A few days later, his body was dug-up by Union Cavalry and was returned to his family.

Buckingham was originally assigned to the Union infantry as a correspondent but had been transferred to cover the Union cavalry operations only a few weeks before the accident.

Buckingham had volunteered at the beginning of the war enlisting into the Fifth Massachusetts regiment and was severely wounded in the first battle of Manassas. Having been declared unfit for active military duty due to his wounds, he volunteered as a correspondent with the *Herald* to write about the war. Buckingham could have stayed home for the rest of the conflict, and told war stories, but instead volunteered to be a war correspondent and lost his life doing it.

HISTORIC SITE IN JOURNALISM
Mt. Zion Old School Baptist Church

In the graveyard adjoining this church, on June 23, 1863, Harpers Illustrated Weekly's Alfred R. Waud, one of the Civil War's most renowned artists, dug the grave for the burial of his friend, Lynde Walter Buckingham, the chief cavalry correspondent for the New York Herald.

Buckingham had spent the day of June 21 covering what would become one of the largest cavalry battles in U.S. history, in and around the villages of Aldie, Middleburg and Upperville. At the front with Union General Judson Kilpatrick throughout the June 21 fight, Buckingham was on his way to Washington with his account of the fighting when Confederate Partisan fighters under Major John Singleton Mosby's command overtook him and caused his horse to dash down a steep hill and throw its rider powerfully to the ground. Buckingham later died of injuries to his skull in a makeshift Union Army hospital within this church.

After burying his friend, Waud rode on to Gettysburg, where on July 2 and 3 he sketched scenes of the fighting there that continue to shape Americans' views of that epic battle. A couple of days after Buckingham's burial, Union Captain Webster, an old friend of his, came to Mt. Zion with an escort and ambulance to disinter the body and send the remains to Buckingham's family.

The Society of Professional Journalists hereby designates Mt. Zion Old School Baptist Church and Graveyard a Historic Site in Journalism. For as long as they exist, they will recall the devotion to duty and fellow man that embody the best qualities of America's war correspondents.

Marked this 14th day of June, 2013.

SOCIETY OF PROFESSIONAL JOURNALISTS.

New York Herald Journalist Lynde Walter Buckingham Marker (N38°57'49" W77°36'44")

29) John Fairfax House *Oak Hill*, June 25 1863 – James Monroe Highway and Oak Hill Farm Road, Leesburg (Private Property)

Front View of *Oak Hill* (N38°59'49″ W77°37'9″)

Ten miles from Leesburg on the Old Carolina Road, today's Route 15, is the historic plantation house *Oak Hill*, the summer home of President James Monroe. Built in 1822, Monroe drafted his famous Monroe Doctrine there in 1823 and in 1825 entertained the Marquis de Lafayette and President John Quincy Adams at this residence during his presidency. The house was designed by Thomas Jefferson.

John W. Fairfax, born June 30, 1828, was a tall, middle-aged man and one of the wealthiest individuals in Northern Virginia when he and his wife Mary Jane bought the *Oak Hill* estate in 1854. His wife was the daughter of Colonel Hamilton Rogers who lived at *Oakham* outside of Middleburg not far from *Oak Hill*.

Although Fairfax had opposed secession, he decided to enlist in the Confederacy and offered his services as a

Confederate Colonel John W. Fairfax

volunteer staff officer. Fairfax sought Lieutenant General James Longstreet who assigned him as a volunteer aide-de-camp and gave him the honorary rank of captain.

Fairfax was a unique character and had a zest for the good things in life and it was not long before the "courtly and rather impressive" Virginian was one of the most popular members on Longstreet's staff. Fairfax was known to be fond of his bottle, his Bible, and baths. On Sundays he would lay down with his bible in one hand and his bottle in the other.

Confederate Lieutenant General James Longstreet

Fairfax's ability to prepare a fine meal and partake in a good poker game were two other things he just loved to do. In addition, Fairfax was a capable, efficient, and brave soldier who was always in the front when involved in any combat engagement. Fairfax even manned an artillery piece replacing the artillerist who had been killed in action. Near Marysville, Tennessee, a reckless Union trooper rode directly into Longstreet's headquarters, so Colonel Fairfax put spurs into his horse, dashed up against the Union interloper, put his pistol to the Union fellows head, and called out "surrender" before the man could even draw his own gun. Fairfax is even mentioned as one of the persons who led Henry Thomas Harrison the "Spy" to General Robert E. Lee's tent when he reported on the movements of the Union army in the Gettysburg campaign. Finally, Fairfax was promoted to lieutenant colonel on January 13, 1865, a few months before the war ended.

Union Major General George G. Meade

While Fairfax was with Longstreet, his wife remained at *Oak Hill* to manage the plantation. On June 25, 1863, she was an unwilling hostess to Union General George G. Meade, the eventual hero of Gettysburg, who made the historic structure his headquarters.

Mrs. Fairfax was on the south side patio talking with General Meade facing toward Aldie when he mentioned how much he wanted to catch the elusive and dangerous Mosby. Mrs. Fairfax then pointed to a lone

John S. Mosby on mount

horseman cutting across the fields to the rear of her property and informed Meade he had just missed his opportunity.

This dwelling was a familiar site to Mosby and his men who visited and operated around this plantation during the last two and a half years of the War Between the States. Mosby and Longstreet both visited *Oak Hill* to see their good friend Colonel Fairfax after the end of the war.

Rear porch of *Oak Hill* where Union General George G. Meade had lunch with Mrs. Fairfax

"Jefferson door" on the rear porch

View from back porch of *Oak Hill*, across the garden, to the field where Mrs. Fairfax referenced Colonel Mosby

View from the field that Major Mosby purportedly rode, to the rear of *Oak Hill*

30) Sutler's Wagon Raid – Mount Gilead on July 20, 1863 – 38906 Mount Gilead Road, Leesburg

Mount Gilead (N39°4'18" W77°39'31")

On July 20, 1863, near Mount Gilead, Mosby captured two heavily-laden sutler's-wagons, a headquarters wagon, fourteen horses, one mule, and forty-five prisoners. Leaving the prisoners and wagons in a hollow under guard, Mosby started back to get more. Seeing a few Union cavalry in a field, the Rangers galloped forward with a yell to attack them, and the Union Cavalry fled towards a piece of woods. Ranger William Hibbs, who was in advance, saw a force of Union infantry in the woods and wheeling his horse called to the rest of the Rangers to come back, but a volley was fired by the Union infantryman before they had time to obey. William was dubbed "Major" Hibbs. The Loudoun Rangers described him as one of Mosby's most desperate characters but not an officer, simply plain "Bill" Hibbs.

A young Ranger named James B. Flynn was shot and fell from his horse, which came out sprinkled with his master's blood. William Hibbs had his horse killed. One of the Yankee prisoners, who was within range, was killed and another fell from his horse and broke his neck as the Rangers were moving off. As for poor Flynn, he would be wounded, captured, and sent to Point Lookout, Maryland.

After the fighting ended, orders were given to push on with the prisoners and horses, and the captured wagons were set on fire. The Rangers had to move very cautiously being completely surrounded. The Rangers often found their way blocked by Union troops. When this happened, the Rangers had to carefully retrace their steps and seek other outlets.

When the Partisans reached the Snickersville Turnpike, a brigade of cavalry was passing, and the Rangers had to fall back and lie close to the ground until they passed. The Rangers succeeded however in getting their captives safely to the Bull Run Mountains. The quantity and quality of the sutler's wagons proved a great treat to the Rangers for they contained all sorts of good things. From the appetizing contents of one, Tom Lake prepared a supper of canned turkey and hot corn bread with a bottle of wine. That was Tom's idea of a feast. He invited his chief Mosby to share the meal, and during its progress Tom was ordered to carry out the forty-five prisoners. The next day, the horses were divided among the

Mosby Ranger Tom Lake (c1895)

Rangers and both the captors and captured started along the mountain side led by Lake with a detail of five or seven men. Together they began to worm their way toward the Southern army at Culpeper.

Asa Moore Janney and Werner Janney who lived in Lincoln, Loudoun County, told a story about a Mosby engagement on Mount Gilead:

> "On an unknown date, an unknown number of Yankees were camped up on Mount Gilead and some of them came down to Summerhill to acquire and search for corn at the farm. That night they would send wagons down for it. That evening Mosby's Partisans were

down by Summerhill and heard the wagons moving. Mosby kept his men ready but held off, watched William Hoge load up the corn, and then attacked the train on their way back to camp. Next morning, Cousin Charley saw the place where the wagons had been burnt. There had been no guard, so Mosby just chased off the wagon drivers. Mosby wasn't a blood-thirsty man, said Cousin Charles. The Yankees came scouring around, but by that time Mosby's men were plowing corn and chopping wood.

Later on, Mosby stopped by the farm and told William Hoge, 'Mr. Hoge, I saw you measuring out the corn and counting off the tally with a candle in your hand. I could have attacked the Yankees then, but I held off, because I knew you were a Union man and it would get you in bad with your own side.'"

It is possible that this story could be referring to Mosby's raid at Mount Gilead on July 20, 1863.

31) Fight with Second Massachusetts Cavalry between Matt Lee's house and Mount Zion Church July 30-31, 1863 – Matt Lee's house, 41631 Olvine Place, Aldie. Mount Zion Church – 40309 John Mosby Highway, Aldie

Mount Zion Church (N38°57'49" W77°36'44")

On Thursday night, July 30, 1863, Mosby with about thirty men raided in the vicinity of Jermantown and Fairfax Court House and captured a number of sutler wagons. They entered Fairfax Court House around ten o'clock and captured one hundred prisoners, one hundred and forty horses and twenty-nine wagons loaded with rich stores and other goods including ice cream. Mosby immediately proceeded to bring them up the Little River Turnpike back to Mosby's Confederacy. This raid would thereafter be referred to as the "Ice Cream Raid."

Having collected all the prizes into one large wagon train, Mosby ordered Joe Calvert, a brave and reliable man, to the front. Calvert was to notify Mosby of any Union force in that direction. Mosby would remain in the rear.

Federal cavalry in Centreville, under the command of Colonel Charles Russell Lowell of the Second Massachusetts Cavalry, had started out after Mosby and his command on a back road in an attempt to intercept the guerillas and recapture the wagons. Lowell was nearer to Aldie than Mosby and his wagons.

Union Colonel Charles R. Lowell

Union Captain George A. Manning

After arriving near Mount Zion Church, Lowell sent Captain George A. Manning and Company M to reach Aldie before Mosby. Lieutenant Goodrich Stone was detailed to catch up with the ambulance train that was moving west on the Little River Turnpike and provide additional armed support. Lieutenant William Manning, the brother of Captain Manning, took twenty men from Company L and guarded the road from Gum Springs to the turnpike. The Union trap was now set.

Moving eight miles up the Little River Turnpike, a Union ambulance-train was spotted by Calvert in the front, guarded by twenty-five cavalry.

"All right," Mosby remarked to Bob Gray, who communicated the information, *"we will just take them too."* At Matt Lee's, just as day was breaking, Mosby rode to the front for the purpose of attacking the ambulance escort when he saw the flash of a pistol. With eight men, the amount of his available force, Mosby dashed forward and found that Ranger Joe Calvert had been

Union Lieutenant William C. Manning

64

attacked and driven back by a party stationed on the road. Bush Underwood, who had been the first to go to Calvert's support, had received a severe saber-cut. The Yankees were then charged, routed, and hotly pursued to within a hundred yards of Mount Zion Church, when Lowell's cavalry appeared in line of battle across the road and at once moved forward.

Lowell's concentrated attack, outnumbering Mosby, forced the rebels to abandon all they had captured—leaving behind all the wagons, horses, prisoners, and other items in their haste to get away. A young gentleman who escaped from the Rangers, stated that Mosby left everything behind except for a wagon load of boots and clothing, which the rebels helped themselves liberally to while they held possession of them.

After the affair, Mosby stated he had one man wounded and captured and really truly lamented losing all those wagons. Lowell reported two men killed and two wounded. A funeral detail was assigned to dig graves for two of the fallen men, Hazen B. Little, a twenty-eight year old printer, and twenty-five year old mason Peter Renard (or Renyard). Both men of the California Battalion were laid to rest under a locust tree in the front yard of the home of Almond Birch near the scene of the conflict. The owner was civil enough to the men who had to carry out this unpleasant chore, bringing them milk and bread, and allowing them to take pears off his tree. See Appendix A, The Almond Birch House.

32) Mosby stopped at *Woodgrove* on way to Loudoun Heights fight on January 9, 1864 – 16860 Woodgrove Road (Intersection of Woodgrove Road and Williams Gap Road), Round Hill (Private Property)

Woodgrove where Mosby stopped before the fight at Loudoun Heights *(*N39°9′6″ W77°46′12″)

At eight o'clock on the night of January 9th 1864, Mosby and his Rangers halted for a few hours at *Woodgrove*, the residence of Mr. Heaton, the father of Ranger Henry Heaton, who provided supper for both the officers and men.

33) Failed night attack Loudoun Heights, Major Henry Cole's Headquarters on January 9th & 10th, 1864 – Branch River Road and Harpers Ferry Road, Loudoun Heights (Private Property)

Union Major Henry Cole's Headquarters at Loudoun Heights (N39°18'53" W77°43'3")

On January 7, 1864, independent Confederate Captain Frank Stringfellow reported to Mosby concerning the situation of Union Major Henry Cole's Maryland Cavalry Battalion of two hundred men, performing picket duty on the Loudoun Heights. This camp was at the eastern base of the Blue Ridge on the road from Hillsboro and Harper's Ferry which Stringfellow thought might be easily surprised and captured, without the firing of a single shot.

Captain Stringfellow was as well-known and reliable a scout and spy as there ever was in the Confederate army. Stringfellow had been employed and trusted by both Robert E. Lee and J.E.B. Stuart for his bravery and for his ability to provide invaluable intelligence concerning the movements of the Union army. Without hesitation, Mosby agreed and prepared for an attack upon Major Cole's camp.

That night, Mosby ordered a meeting of the whole command at Upperville for the next day at twelve o'clock. The men were reluctant to leave their comfortable log fires. The mercury read zero at breakfast that morning and the snow was one foot deep on the ground with a fair prospect of another fall of snow during the day. Only one hundred men reported for duty.

Confederate Scout & Spy Frank Stringfellow

At three o'clock on the afternoon of the 9th of January, orders were given to mount and fall into a line of march. At eight o'clock at nightfall, the Rangers halted for a few hours at *Woodgrove*, the residence of Mr. Heaton, the father of Ranger Henry Heaton, whose cheerful fires blazed in every room. A nice supper had been prepared for both officers and men. Several hours pleasantly passed away until a courier arrived from Stringfellow (who, with a party of ten men had remained to watch the camp) with the information that everything was favorable for the execution of the plan.

At ten o'clock, Mosby's men were ordered to resume the march, taking the high road to Harper's Ferry alternately riding and walking to keep their feet and hands from freezing as well as keeping their entire bodies warm. While riding, the Rangers would put the reins in their mouths and their hands under the saddle-blankets next to the horse's skins to keep from being frozen. The night was clear but intensely cold, and the snow lay six inches deep on the ground, muffling the sound of the horse's feet as the column moved.

Major Mosby's brother William Mosby commented about the raid to Loudoun Heights:

> *"The snow covered the ground, an icy wind swept down through the passes of the neighboring Blue Ridge, and altogether the night was the coldest that ever broke away from the North Pole and wandered south of the Arctic circle—a splendid night for a surprise party. As the long column slowly threaded its way through the chilly darkness, we rapidly began to freeze up. Men would complain and then sink into that lethargic indifference that comes from utter chill. Several were badly frostbitten, but they kept on the march. The bridle reins would fall from my numb hands unnoticed, until the unguided horse drew my attention to the fact."*

Mosby Ranger William Mosby

Within a mile and a half of the camp, Mosby's men were joined by Stringfellow's party and leaving the grade, the raiders struck across a narrow skirt of country in single file until they reached the base of the Short Hills. Here the command was halted and the horses fed while Mosby, accompanied by Stringfellow, went forward to reconnoiter the camp.

In about two hours when they returned, the Confederate column marched along the base of the mountain until it reached the Potomac River. Subsequently, the Rangers proceeded along the river bank toward Harper's Ferry ascending on the route; a wooded cliff which could only be done by leading the horses single file, grasping the thick bushes with which it was covered. Along the crest of this cliff ran the grade which the Rangers gained at a point midway between Harper's Ferry and where the camp fires of several thousand Union troops were quartered on the opposite side of the river.

The Rangers also saw the camp which Mosby and Stringfellow wished to surprise. At around five o'clock, Mosby with one hundred and ten men stood there in almost the very center of the strongest fortified post in all the line of defenses around Harper's Ferry. The Union camp was buried in profound sleep and not a sentry was awake. On reaching that point, Mosby was sure that the capture of the camp of the enemy was a certainty. Everything so far seemed to predict a monumental success and a great victory for the Rangers. That positive forecast however, would never come to fruition.

William Mosby continued his story:

> "By the time we reached Loudoun Heights and silently formed to attack there was nothing but ice in my boots. I had to lift each leg by manual strength and carefully replace the frozen feet in the stirrups for a securer footing. When it came to pulling off my gloves, preparatory to drawing my revolvers—we always went into a fight with a gun in each hand, bare of gloves for greater efficiency – I found my fingers too cold for the task, and had to slowly work them off with the chattering teeth. That done, it was like bending bones to get those stiff and icy fingers gripped around the butts of the revolvers."

Not a cloud could be seen. The moon seemed to shine with her silvery light brighter than ever before. The air was still and piercing cold. Mosby made his dispositions for attack.

Richard Montjoy was sent down the Hillsboro road about one quarter of a mile with six men to secure the picket of Cole's Second Maryland Cavalry at a bridge over the Branch River, giving Mosby an escape route if needed. It would be the smartest move Mosby would make. Captain Billy Smith, with a few men, was directed to secure the horses which were standing around the hospital building. Stringfellow with his scouts was sent to capture Major Cole and the other officers at his headquarters which was in a two story house on the edge of the camp by the side of a mountain, while Mosby with the bulk of the command were to attack the sleeping camp.

In order to make the surprise complete, Mosby dismounted a portion of the men, and had succeeded in capturing the first row of tents where Cole's men lay sleeping when for some almost unaccountable means the sudden crack of a pistol rang out. A shot was fired alarming all in the camp of an intruder. No one knows who fired the shot or where it came from. It could have been inadvertently fired by one of Mosby's own men, or a Union sentinel who happened to see Stringfellow or Mosby's men in the camp. Nevertheless, everyone now knew something was amiss.

Upon hearing the shot, Mosby ordered a charge into the nearest tents. William Mosby added, *"Then came the command, 'Charge!' With the words we were flashing through the pickets and sweeping like a whirlwind through the camp of the astonished enemy."*

Above the din rang out the clear voices of Smith and Lieutenant Tom Turner, *"Charge them, boys! Charge them!"* About thirty Rangers ran into the tents firing indiscriminately with their pistols. The enemy soon cried out, *"The camp is yours! We surrender! Stop firing!"* And the firing ceased.

The initial firing scared the Union pickets so much at the bridge Montjoy had been sent to secure, that they fled from their assigned posts to the nearby woods before Montjoy could even reach them. Stringfellow and his men actually made it to Cole's headquarters and entered at the front door of the house, but Cole had made his escape from the rear of the building into the mountain and then hastened back to the camp to help rally his men. Captain Francis Gallagher, suffering from a broken leg in an adjoining room, escaped unnoticed.

Union Major Henry A. Cole

Subsequently, Stringfellow's party started back from Cole's quarters with nothing to show for it, and contrary to orders, came galloping towards Mosby's men. Mosby supposing them to be Union cavalry ordered his men to fire killing or wounding several of them before the mistake was discovered. Captain John Robinson, a Scotchman riding with Stringfellow and a former captain in the English army, had been killed by Mosby's own men on their return through the camp. Private Mason Owens was also killed by friendly fire.

Lieutenant Turner had fallen at the first fire while advancing towards the tents when a ball struck him. He threw up his hands exclaiming, *"I am shot!"* Two Rangers caught him and holding him on his horse, led him off the field mortally wounded.

The firing and the confusion which began to prevail roused the Maryland cavalrymen from their tents and they poured a most murderous fire into Mosby's Rangers. Ranger William E. Colston, a brave young Baltimorean, had fallen while trying to rally the men and fell immediately in front of a Union tent belonging to Union Sergeant C. Armour Newcomer. Ranger Fount Beattie had his horse shot and he himself received a ball in his thigh.

Mosby Ranger William E. Colston

Armour Newcomer, Second Union Maryland Cavalry

Union Captain George W.F. Vernon continued to rally his men and directed them to fire at anyone mounted. A cry soon rang out on the cold frosty air, *"Shoot every soldier on horseback."* It was hand to hand and a perfect hell! Cole's cavalrymen were using their carbines to good effect. Captain Vernon discharged the last load from his second revolver when he fell with a ghastly wound in the head.

During the fight every

Mosby Ranger Fount Beattie

man on both sides was fighting for his life. Mosby, seeing that the situation was becoming critical and that his men were falling beneath the fire of friends as well as the enemy and hearing the signal – gun on Loudoun Heights, ordered a retreat in the direction of Hillsboro. But, this order was not heard by those on the outskirts of the camp.

Union Captain George W. F. Vernon

In a little while, Confederate Captain Billy Smith, riding with Captain William Chapman, dashed in among the tents with fifty men, but was soon driven out. The two officers, then returned to

Mosby Ranger Captain William Chapman

the camp to look after their wounded and had not gone far when they recognized Charles Paxson of Loudoun, extended on the ground so badly wounded that he was unable to rise. He besought them in moving terms to carry him off, *"For God's sake not to leave him."* Captain Smith, hearing the appeal, suddenly whirled his horse around, and reached down to pull up the dying youth in front of him to bring him off. Smith was shot in the heart by a Yankee in one of the tents a short distance away instantly killing him. Chapman, supposing his

Mosby Ranger Charles Paxson

companion was only wounded, hastened to give assistance to bear him away. Chapman caught Smith and disengaging Smith's feet from the stirrups, laid him on the ground. Unfortunately, Chapman was met by Lieutenant Bob Gray who told him Mosby had ordered a retreat. Chapman, now informed of Mosby's order and also receiving heavy gunfire, was compelled to leave Smith and rejoin the command.

Mosby gathered up his shattered forces and retired from this disastrous attack in the direction of Hillsboro where Montjoy had secured the road. They had not proceeded more than a few hundred yards toward Hillsboro when they overtook Baron Von Massow, who touched with a generous compassion, had just lifted a wounded soldier on his horse to convey him to a place of safety.

At this time, two miles farther on, Mosby was standing by the bedside of Lieutenant Tom Turner who had been mortally wounded early in the fight and had been borne to the house of Levi Waters, a local citizen, which stood on the side of the road. It was a heart rending spectacle to see the men gathered around the wounded officer to look for the last time upon the one whom they had followed in so many fights, but Turner assured his sorrowing comrades that in another week he would be with them again. It was not to be. Turner would linger five days, receiving every attention from the Southern people in the neighborhood could provide, before he passed away. Turner, a brave and courageous man, was known amongst the men as "Fighting Tom."

Consequently, the loss of Smith and the grief Mosby felt when told of his death could not be better evidenced than by his crying like a child and declining to do anything for a month. The sorrow Mosby manifested at the loss of Smith was shared by the men and other officers. William "Billy" Smith was brave and generous to a fault. His men idolized him. His conversation was that of a frank and generous nature which captivated everyone who met him.

The Rangers brought off ten prisoners and forty-five horses which the enemy had just drawn from the Quartermaster—a poor compensation for the grievous loss of Smith, Turner, Owens, Paxson, Colston, Robinson, and William H. Turner of Maryland; while Boyd Smith, Beattie, Henry Edmonds, and several others had received less serious injuries. Ranger Leonard Brown was taken the next morning attempting to bring out two horses and one prisoner.

Mosby Ranger Boyd Smith

The command reached *Woodgrove* by sunrise the next morning from which place a flag of truce was sent to Major Cole by Captain William Chapman and Montjoy to propose an exchange of prisoners and request permission to remove the command's dead and wounded. But Major Cole refused to receive any communication from Mosby which showed the embittered feelings of the enemy towards Mosby.

While Cole declined to give Mosby the bodies, he did tell Chapman that any citizen or member of the family could come and get them. A day or two afterwards, Captain Smith's wife, father, and mother went to Loudoun Heights. On their arrival at Cole's headquarters, an order was received from Brigadier General James A. Mulligan, the commander of the post, to arrest them. The family remained under arrest for forty-eight hours.

General Mulligan declined to see them or even hold any communication with them. Finally an interview was obtained with one of the adjutants of the post, but before he would consent to give her the body of her husband, Mrs. Smith was compelled to go down on her knees.

In the meanwhile, the enemy had robbed Captain Smith of his money, watch, papers, and anything else, and had absolutely taken every vestige of clothing from his body except his drawers. The bodies of Colston, Robinson, Paxson, and the two others were served in the same way; all of them buried in a sink. Before Mrs. Smith could see the body of her husband, it had to be carried to the river and washed. Not only did the commandant of the post arrest Mrs. Smith's father and mother, but he threatened to place under arrest Major Cole and all of his officers for not sending Captain Chapman and Montjoy under arrest to his headquarters. General Mulligan, however, never carried his threat into execution.

Union Brigadier General James A. Mulligan

Major Cole telegraphed to Washington, *"He was attacked that morning before daylight by Colonel Mosby, Colonel White, and part of Rosser's Brigade; and after an hour's desperate fighting the enemy were driven back and routed with heavy loss in killed, wounded, and prisoners."* The fight did not last fifteen minutes. The Marylanders lost six killed and fourteen wounded including Captain Vernon seriously and Lieutenant John Rivers slightly wounded.

The loss of Smith, Turner, Paxson, Colston, and the others, was a severe blow to Mosby and cast a gloom over Mosby's Confederacy when it was known. The spirits of the men were in a measure broken and although Smith and Turner were succeeded by able and brave officers, it was a long time before they enjoyed the same esteem and confidence that were given to Smith and Turner. Charles Paxson was one of the most promising young men in the battalion, and had he lived, would have definitely distinguished himself.

Cole's men, initially surprised by Mosby, had fought gallantly in the snow, many of them with nothing on except their underclothing. They were glad to have an opportunity to dress and as many of them jokingly remarked, they did not mind the fighting so much but the next time that Mosby came, they would thank him to send word so they would have an opportunity to dress and be in proper condition to receive company. General Mulligan sent Major Cole twenty gallons of whiskey to be distributed among the men. The men greatly accepted the gift and drank to the good general's health.

William Mosby further spoke about his experience after the encounter at Loudoun Heights:

> *"My hands were fairly tingling with heat, my feet throbbing hot with the boiling blood coursing through them, and my body so oppressively warm that I flung wide my overcoat to get relief. In short, I was fairly burning up. Yes, for that chilly feeling,"* added Mr. Mosby, *"there is nothing like a stiff fight at close quarters with revolvers. It beats the best heating system ever invented."*

Thus sadly ended one of Mosby's most daring enterprises, which promised to be a perfect success, but ended up one of his greatest military mistakes. The defeat at Loudoun Heights was enough to dampen the ardor of any spirit, even Mosby's.

Afterwards, Mosby blamed Stringfellow for this resounding defeat and Stringfellow blamed Mosby. They would never talk to each other again. In a letter, dated April 4th, 1915, a little over one year before he died, Mosby wrote, *"...Then I am afraid if I talk about myself I may get up the reputation of telling fabulous stories as Frank Stringfellow did. Most of Frank's tales would have been equally true if told of the Argonaut. He was a brave soldier, but a great liar."*

Mosby never forgave Frank Stringfellow!

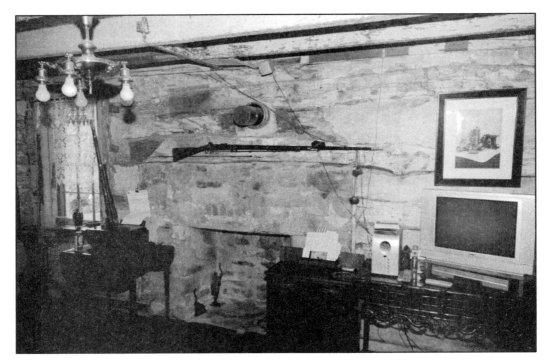
Interior fireplace on Cole's Headquarters where he escaped

34) Failed night attack Loudoun Heights, Picket Post on January 10, 1864 – Branch River Road and Harpers Ferry Road, Loudoun Heights

It is at this bridge where Richard Montjoy scared away the Union pickets of Major Henry Cole's Maryland Cavalry Battalion to give Mosby an escape route to Hillsboro when he retreated from Loudoun Heights (N39°16′3″ W77°43′34″)

35) Failed night attack Loudoun Heights, Highway Marker on January 10, 1864 – Branch River Road and Harpers Ferry Road, Loudoun Heights

Loudoun Heights Fight marker (N39°18′59″ W77°43′1″)

36) Levi Waters House, where Tom Turner died January 11, 1864 – Harpers Ferry Road and Pine Hill Lane, Hillsboro (Private Property)

Levi Waters House (N39°17′42″ W77°43′14″)

Approximately two miles from Loudoun Heights, still stands the ruins of the home belonging to Levi Waters. It was there where Mosby and his men deposited their gallant Lieutenant Tom Turner who was mortally wounded on the morning of January 10, 1864 in the raid against Cole's cavalry at Loudoun Heights.

Mosby stood by the bedside of Lieutenant Turner and was deeply affected by the spectacle of seeing his men gathered around the wounded officer to look for the last time at the officer they had followed in so many fights; but the men still had hope because Turner kept assuring his dejected comrades that in another week he would be with them again.

Mosby Ranger Tom Turner. Courtesy of Eric Buckland

Almost a week later, a Union sympathizer living near Levi Waters reported to Cole's headquarters that a severely wounded officer in Mosby's command had been left at a farm. Sergeant C. Armor Newcomer was ordered to take a squad of men to the farmer's house after dark and bring the wounded man to camp. On arriving at their destination, Newcomer found everything as the citizen had said. Newcomer described Lieutenant Turner as a man much larger than the average size, a fine specimen of manhood, and perhaps twenty-five years of age. Newcomer also stated that Turner had been shot in the breast, the ball going clear through his body and it was evident he would not live.

Newcomer spoke to Turner kindly and told him his orders were to bring him to camp. However, if he would give his word of honor as a soldier and gentleman, not to leave the farmhouse without first notifying Major Cole, Newcomer, would assume responsibility and permit him to remain where he was. Newcomer further went on and said that Turner grasped his hand and thanked him, and said he did not see how one of Cole's men could be so kind to one of Mosby's command after trying to attack them in their beds. Newcomer supposedly told him to think no more of worldly affairs, but turn his thoughts to heaven and ask forgiveness from God, the Great Father of all. Newcomer returned to camp without Turner, and on the following day he received word that the lieutenant was dead.

Unfortunately, Turner would never again mount his fighting steed; nor ever again listen to the trumpet's call to assemble; nor follow his guerilla chieftain into battle. Turner's body would be buried in two or three different locations before finally coming to rest in the Union Cemetery in Leesburg.

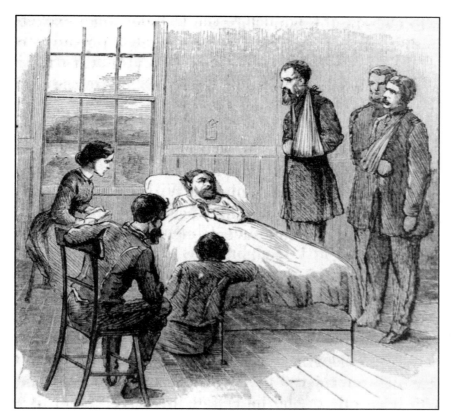

Death of Mosby Ranger Tom Turner at Levi Waters' house

37) Union deserter Pony Ormsby captured by Second Massachusetts Cavalry on February 5-7, 1864 – Aldie Mill, 39401 John Mosby Highway, Aldie

On January 24, 1865, William E. "Pony" Ormsby deserted Company E, Second Massachusetts Cavalry and disappeared into Mosby's Confederacy. He was a baggage handler before the war and was supposedly induced by a southern belle to desert the Union army and ride with the notorious guerrilla chieftain John S. Mosby.

On Saturday, February 5, 1864, a patrol belonging to the Second Massachusetts Cavalry returned to camp that evening with the Union deserter Private Ormsby, who had left his post as picket guard at Lewinsville in Fairfax County some weeks ago. Ormsby was dressed in a Confederate uniform, armed with two pistols, and he was accused of leading an enemy cavalry charge against the Union rear guard of a column of the Second Massachusetts Cavalry while it was passing through the village of Aldie. A Court Martial was immediately ordered to be held for the very next day.

On February 6, 1864, at five o'clock in the afternoon, a Drum Head Court Martial was convened charging Ormsby with desertion to the enemy. After various witnesses testified to seeing Ormsby firing his weapon against the Union patrol. Ormsby issued the following statement on his own behalf:

"I had no idea of leaving this place to join any rebel command at all. I deserted from here to go home and see my parents. My mother was in Boston the last time I heard from her and she wished me to get a furlough and come home to see her. They expected her in New York. I took the horses away from here, I were going to sell them to get money to go home on. When I got out at Aldie there was three of Mosby's men met me and they took my horses and arms from me. I were taken from there up above Middleburg and left with a southern lady but yesterday morning they came to where I was and a young fellow wished me to go down with him to his house. He lived below Aldie and I was acquainted down there with some ladies. I was going down to see them and before I met another young man named Davis and he wanted me to go over between the two Pikes with him and get some liquor; and I went over with him and I got drunk and we followed down between the Pikes to very near where they come together at Aldie.

Just before we came to Aldie we met a wagon and one of the men rode up to it and asked them if they saw any Yankees, and I don't recollect the answer he gave him. And just as we passed the wagon I heard somebody coming up behind and I saw five more men – I knew two of them – They were brothers and their names were Underwood and one them asked a Negro if he had seen any Yankees around and he said he had seen nine.

And Davis rode up to my side then and he pulled out his revolver… and fired – I drew my revolver and cocked it and it went off. Then I turned in my saddle and fired off up the hill. I was so drunk that I couldn't see nothing at all. And I turned down and tried to jump a creek but my horse couldn't jump it and I got off on foot. I could scarcely stand up I was so intoxicated. When we were over at the house where we got the liquor one of the boys asked me to come down to Aldie with him. I told him I wouldn't without arms. He told me to come over to Middleburg with me and he'd get me some. I went and he gave me a horse and two revolvers. I saw Mosby twice and he promised to give me a pass Monday to go into Texas or he'd set me across the river at Point of Rocks. I know I done wrong and I'm sorry for it and I think I was always counted a sober man when I was here and always done my duty very well until I got into a scrape about a horse trade down here. That's what caused me to desert more than anything because I had my pay taken away from me."

The Court was then closed, and after mature deliberation upon the evidence declared Private William E. Ormsby guilty of the specification and ordered him to be shot to death. The Chaplain of the Second Massachusetts Cavalry was a participant of Ormsby's execution and recorded the following statement:

"The hardest duty that ever fell to my lot as Chaplain was to prepare a deserter to die. He was one of our own regiment, and born in Massachusetts, but had early in life gone to California, where he led a wild and reckless career till he enlisted and came East. Now he had yielded to the fascinations of a Southern girl and been induced to desert, and was captured while fighting against us with a band of guerillas.

This offense was of course unpardonable in martial law; yet, as he chose me for his counsel at the trial by drum-head court martial, I pleaded, in extenuation, his youth and the blandishments of the Southern beauty, but to no effect. Perhaps one reason why I did not win the case that the opposing counsel was Lewis S. Dabney, whose legal acumen made him then Judge Advocate, and later made him one of the leaders of the Bar in Boston. Still I had to admit in my own mind that in the existing military situation the sentence of death must be pronounced. The poor victim chose to lean on my arm as he walked to execution behind his own coffin borne by his old messmates, while the band marched beside playing a funeral dirge. And he leaned still more closely on my faith that, though his country could not forgive him, beset as she was with enemies, God would forgive if he was truly penitent; and the thought appealed to the native nobleness of his nature, and awoke in him the desire even then to redeem himself and to serve the cause that he had betrayed and the more he revolved this in his mind, the more he felt the inspiration of noble feeling, and, being permitted to speak a few last words to his fellow soldiers who were drawn up on three sides of a hollow square to witness the execution, he said:

'Comrades! I want to acknowledge that I am guilty and that my punishment is just. But I want also that you should know that I did not desert because I lost faith in our cause. I believe we are on the right side, and I think it will succeed. But take warning from my example, and whatever comes do not desert the old flag for which I am proud to die.'

Everything now being ready, I offered prayer with him and commended him to the mercy of God; then I bound the handkerchief over his eyes, and at his request asked the marksmen to aim steadily and at his heart. Then shaking hands with him in farewell, I said, "Now die like a man.'

He sat down upon the foot of his coffin in perfect composure, and said, 'I am ready.' Fronting him were six men in line, with carbines, five of which were loaded. Each man could persuade himself that his own carbine was the unloaded one, and so was relieved from the other necessary conclusion that he had shot this fellow.

The sergeant in command gave the order – 'Ready! Aim! Fire!' and the deserter in one moment was dead. The lesson of his punishment had never to be repeated in our brigade."

Pony Ormsby was buried at the site of the execution presumably on Ayre Hill, in Vienna, in Fairfax County. The whereabouts of his grave would remain a mystery to historians until the twenty-first century, when a local historian found that he had been dug-up after the war and his remains had been moved to Arlington National Cemetery.

Pony Ormsby's Grave at Arlington National Cemetery (N38°52′48″ W77°04′12″)

38) Mosby attends a wedding at Johnson's Chapel on February 6, 1864 – 20568 Airmont Road, Bloomfield

Johnson's Chapel, built in 1857, now called "Old Chapel" (N39°3′12″ W77°49′12″)

On February 6, 1864, Mosby and eighteen to twenty of his men attended a wedding at the Johnson's Chapel in Bloomfield. Mosby termed it the "objective point" to his men, and arrived a half hour before the festivities were scheduled to begin. Upon entering the church, Mosby and his men were gracefully greeted by the hostess of the event, the charming and dignified Mrs. Kate Powell Carter from *Oatlands*, a bride of a few weeks herself. Mosby knew her as a steadfast friend of himself and his partisan battalion. After taking off his wrappings and overcoat, he and his men joined the festivities.

Other than her responsibility of taking care of the guests of the wedding, Mrs. Carter decided she had another mission for the event; to procure a chaplain for Mosby and his men. Her feelings were that some of Mosby's men were possibly being killed every day, and they needed a suitable parson to tend to them. She set her sights on the chaplain for the wedding, the Reverend Adolphus Adam.

Mrs. Kate Powell Carter from Oatlands

She discussed the need for a parson with Mosby who agreed that should a suitable person be found who demonstrated the higher qualities of a missionary – the piety, learning, zeal, courage and the force of character to be able to impress the consciences of this group of his men; he would provide them with a religious instructor. Mrs. Carter couldn't agree more. Throughout the evening, she discussed the matter with the Reverend Adam and felt she was making substantial progress. That was until the music began for dancing after the ceremony.

Thinking she had convinced the reverend he was the best man for the job, she was deeply disappointed when Reverend Adam made straight for one of the fairest young ladies in attendance, Miss Josephine Stevenson. Reverend Adam proceeded to dance with her, but also proceeded to dance a wild solo creating a great clatter with his feet.

Mrs. Carter was greatly mortified at the display not realizing the good Reverend had partaken in a half pint of "blockade" which had loosened his inhibitions for his behavior in such a proper setting. Furthermore, Adam repeatedly yelled at the musicians to play one "hell-bender" after another.

Burying her face in a handkerchief and weeping, she was only consoled by the assurances of Colonel Mosby that this reverend would never be associated with his command which restored her smile and countenance. Nevertheless, Adolphus Adam is listed in the regimental of Mosby's Rangers as their chaplain.

39) Second Fight at Blakely's Grove on February 20, 1864 – Greengarden and Millville Roads, Upperville

On Saturday, February 20, 1864, Major Mosby, Jake Lavender, Johnny Edmonds, and John Munson, were seated at a table eating breakfast at the home of Joseph Blackwell. Suddenly, a little boy named Jimmy Edmonds ran in and said that the turnpike, which was about a mile distant, was *"full of Yankees."* At first, they were incredulous, but Mosby said they had better saddle up and see for themselves. When they reached the road they discovered that it was crowded, just as the little boy had said, with Union cavalry which turned out to be two hundred and fifty troopers. The cavalry belonged to Major Henry Cole's Battalion on a march from their camp at Harper's Ferry to Front Royal.

Cole's Battalion had made a raid through Loudoun and Fauquier Counties, capturing several of Mosby's men. Cole made it as far as Piedmont, on the Virginia Midland Road, before he started to return.

Cole then proceeded to Mrs. Chappelier's orchard, where Mosby had followed them and determined to open fire---with Edmonds and Munson each being armed with a long-range rifle. This unexpected attack upon the Marylanders column necessitated a change of plan by Major Cole. Instead of staying the course which lay through the Blue Ridge Mountains, he reversed the head of his column and returned toward Upperville. As Cole approached Gap Run, Mosby, with his three men took position on a hill immediately above the ford. It was here where Mosby grabbed Edmonds' carbine and he and Munson fired into the Union column.

Mosby and his three men wounded a man, killed a horse, and quickly increased the speed of the retreating party. This irregular fighting was kept up until the Marylanders reached Upperville, with the Partisans gaining strength and men along the route.

At this place, Major Cole halted to have his horses fed; a pause which proved very advantageous to Mosby, for during that interval, fifty of his men gathered around him. The mode of attack was now changed from sharp-shooting on the hills to assaults on the enemy's rear, which induced Major Cole to keep out a strong rear guard of sharp-shooters. About two miles farther on Mosby charged the rear guard, drove three of them in, throwing the column into some confusion. He soon scattered before Cole ordered a counter-charge.

As soon as Cole resumed the march, the Rangers again charged, and this time with success. By getting into close quarters, the Rangers drove Cole and his men as far as Blakely's Grove School House. In this charge, Richard Montjoy encountered Union Captain William L. Morgan and

Union Major Henry A. Cole

after a personal contest in view of both commands, killed him. Mosby witnessed the duel and in warm terms congratulated the victor when it was over assuring him that he had that day won a commission.

It was at Blakely's Grove School House where Cole made his stand. At the school house, the fighting was very animated, charging and countercharging until the enemy took refuge behind the stone fences which formed the crossroads at that place. Using these as a breast work, they continued the fight until Mosby, resolving not to be held at such disadvantage, flanked their position as if to throw himself in their front.

While executing this movement, he was brought in full range of the enemy who having identified him among the assailants opened upon him a concentrated fire. Mosby's appearance was conspicuous, dressed in a dark overcoat, a cape lined with scarlet which was thrown over his shoulder, and a light felt hat with a black plume. He was mounted on a grey horse, remarkable for its beauty and activity. Major Cole offered a reward to anyone who would kill the Partisan chief.

Major Cole however, realizing the dangerous position in which he had been, resumed his retreat. His flanks and rear were still exposed however to galling attacks which were kept up for several miles farther. The Rangers followed Cole as far as Bloomfield, and there gave up the chase. Mosby's wounded were Lieutenant Frank Fox, Alexander Spinks, and Starke. Major Cole lost one officer and six privates killed, and eight men, with their horses and equipments, taken prisoners. The Marylanders carried most of their wounded---one however, shot through the head, lingered some time at the school house at Blakely's Grove, but died and was buried in the fence corner. Mosby found two of their dead near Bloomfield a week after the fight, half eaten up by hogs.

During their advance through Fauquier, Cole captured two Rangers, John and Bartlett Bolling at the residence of their father, and killed Joseph McCobb of Baltimore. Surprised at his boarding-house, McCobb mounted his horse and while attempting to leap a fence, was thrown and killed. William A. Brawner and J.W. Coiner inadvertently rode into a party of Cole's men near Upperville, mistaking them for Rangers, and were quickly taken prisoner. Montjoy and George H. Ayre had their horses shot.

Mosby Ranger William A. Brawner

When the Rangers were chasing Cole's cavalry through Upperville, the boys' school was dismissed for recess. One very fat boy took in the situation at once and jumped on his pony with his McGuffy's Third Reader for his only weapon, which he waved aloft. He dashed into the chase with Mosby

83

and his men, whooping and yelling and never stopping until all the Rangers had quit the chase.

That day was the boy's last at school, for he insisted on joining Mosby's command and, until the end of the war, was one of the gamest and best soldiers Mosby had. He was Henry Cabell "Cab" Maddux, known to every man in the command and to everybody in Mosby's Confederacy as a fighter.

Before disbanding the command after the fight at Blakely School House, Major Mosby ordered it to rendezvous at Piedmont the next day, for the purpose of escorting the remains of McCobb to his final resting place.

Mosby Ranger Cab Maddux

40) Engagement at Second Dranesville, Anker's Shop on February 21-22, 1864 – 21200 Campus Drive, Sterling

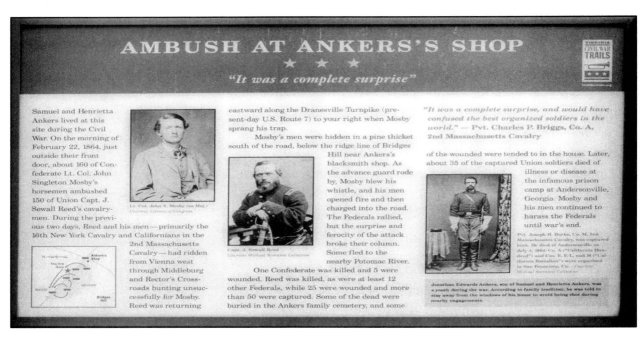

Marker at Anker's Shop (N39°1'36" W77°23'36")

On Sunday, February 21, 1864, Mosby called for a command to gather at Piedmont for the funeral of Joseph McCobb. McCobb had been killed at his boarding place by Cole's Union Cavalry. Trying to get away, McCobb mounted his horse and jumped a fence and was thrown violently to the ground and killed. At around nine o'clock in the morning the Rangers started to arrive to show their respects. Over two hundred men would eventually assemble for McCobb's final rites.

A few hours before noon, the funeral was interrupted by news that a scouting party composed of a hundred and fifty-men of the Second Massachusetts Cavalry and a platoon of the Sixteenth New York Cavalry was at Rector's Crossroads. This expedition was commanded by Union Captain J. Sewell Reed, made up of one hundred and twenty-five men from the regiment and twenty-five men from the Sixteenth New York Cavalry. The Yankees were piloted on their raid by the notorious Charlie Binns, a deserter from Mosby's command.

Union Captain J. Sewell Reed

Mosby immediately ordered Captain William Chapman to take a hundred and fifty men and find Reed who was heading towards Mountsville. Mosby then ordered Sam Underwood and another Ranger to follow Reed's line of march, and report back to him where they were going. Without knowing Reed's assigned course of action, Mosby correctly anticipated the route that Reed would use to return to Fairfax County.

Mosby Ranger Samuel L. Underwood

Union Major Douglas Frazar

At two a.m. on Monday, February 22, 1864, on George Washington's Birthday, Reed and his troopers camped for the night at the Belmont farm, owned by George Kephart and located about five miles east of Leesburg. Underwood reported back to Mosby and informed him that Reed had linked up with a body of cavalry commanded by Major Douglas Frazar, of the Sixteenth New York Cavalry. Mosby ordered Chapman to move his men to Guilford Station near Anker's Shop on the Dranesville Turnpike. It is here where Mosby decided to set up an ambush.

Anker's Shop Foundation

Stone Marker on Site of Anker's Family Home and Cemetery

Arriving at the site on the Dranesville Turnpike, Mosby sent Walter Whaley to watch for Captain Reed. If Reed took the side road back to Fairfax, the Rangers would be able to intercept them. Mosby wanted to attack Reed at the front, rear, and the flank. Company A, with part of Company B, under Lieutenant Franklin Williams from Fairfax County, were positioned along the edge of a thick pine woods in columns of fours to charge in their front. Company C, with the balance of

Mosby Ranger Walter Whaley

Company B, under Captain William Chapman, were to charge in their rear; while Richard Montjoy was given fifteen to twenty men armed with carbines and posted in the pines along the road between Williams and Chapman. Mosby ordered Frank "Red Fox" Rahm and another Ranger to go further down the road to allow them to be easily seen and to act as decoys, to attract the advancing column's vanguard.

Mosby Ranger Franklin Williams

Mosby Ranger Lieutenant Frank H. Rahm

After all arrangements had been made, Mosby told his Rangers, *"Men, the Yankees are coming and it is very likely we will have a hard fight. When you are ordered to charge, I want you to go right through them. Reserve your fire until you get close enough to see clearly what you are shooting at and let every shot tell."*

As the Rangers were waiting in their concealed positions, Whaley dashed up with the information that the Union column had separated---Major Frazar having taken the country road, but that Captain Reed with the California Battalion, was traveling directly towards them.

As soon as the Union raiders arrived at Anker's Shop, which is on the slope of the hill toward Leesburg, where the Rangers were posted, the advance Union guard numbering about twenty men saw the decoy "Red Fox" in the middle of the road. The Union vanguard immediately charged in pursuit of Rahm, but the officer in charge, possibly sensing something wrong, stopped his men right in front of Montjoy's hidden rifleman.

Mosby fearing discovery, realized he couldn't wait any longer and blew his silver whistle initiating the fight, followed by the crack of Montjoy's carbines. Many Union saddles were emptied by the initial volley. Mosby charged at the head of William's detachment down the hill upon the front of Reed's column, while Captain Chapman took a circuitous route through the pines and fell upon the rear.

As soon as the attack was initiated, resistance on the part of the enemy was of a short duration. The surprised prey scattered and fled in every direction, with the bulk of them racing toward Leesburg closely pursued by the hot blooded Rangers.

Captain Reed tried to rally his men, but it was useless. Some of Reed's men were driven into the Potomac River. Dead and drowned bodies were found for several days afterward. Charlie Binns was recognized immediately by many of Mosby's men and made a great escape pushing his horse as fast as he could knowing if he was caught he was a goner.

Mosby Deserter Charlie Binns

Mosby Ranger Johnny Munson

Ranger John Munson had this to say about Mosby in the fight, *"I saw him weaving in and out of the fighting mass like a ferret!"* Ranger Marshall Crawford said in his memoir, *"Desperate was the fighting and terrible was "the slaughter; with a large portion of the fighting being hand to hand."*

James Chappalear, who was riding on his first raid under Mosby, was shot off his horse. Ranger Monroe Robinson seeing Chappalear fall, rode up to the Yankee who shot him and killed him instantly. Ranger John Munson was shot in the back near his spine. He claimed that a Yankee surrendered and when he motioned him to leave the field the cavalryman shot him in the back. Ludwell Lake in turn killed the Union back shooter!

Mosby Ranger Ludwell Lake (c1895)

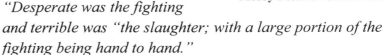

Mosby Ranger James Pendleton Chappalear

The same thing happened to Baron Von Massow, a Prussian officer serving with Mosby and earnestly involved in the fighting at Anker's Shop. Von Massow, with his hat waving a big ostrich plume dashed into the fray with an old German saber flashing in the light. He saw Captain Reed and charged him emptying his revolver and finally swinging his saber preparing to do battle. But Reed thought the best of it and threw up his arms.

But, as soon as Reed passed Von Massow, he turned and shot him in the back. Captain Chapman witnessing Reed's cowardly deed rode up and shot him in the forehead. The brave Californian tried to lift his weapon for another shot, found his strength failing, and plunged forward on his face, with his body falling very near the severely injured Von Massow. After the fight Chapman wrote, *"...when I came back to him he {Von Massow}, was lying on the grass suffering fearfully, sure that he was dying. I thought I would cheer him up by telling him that the man who had wounded him had been disposed of, so I said: 'Von Massow, probably you will be pleased to know that I have killed the man who wounded you.' Suffering terribly though he*

Mosby Ranger Barron Von Massow

was, Von Massow raised himself upon his elbow, saluted, and said to me with profound courtesy: 'I am very much obliged to you.'" The brave German pulled through after a long and hard siege and made up his mind to return to his native land. After returning to Europe he would later command the Ninth Cavalry Corps, which was the crack Corps of the German Army during World War I.

Ranger Johnny Edmonds was also wounded. However, he was an example of divine intervention. When he left his house to attend McCobb's funeral, his mother insisted that he take a bible. Edmonds placed the good book in his trousers and forgot about it. During the fight, a bullet hit Edmonds in his thigh. However, the bullet spent all of its force passing through the bible before lodging against his leg bone. Had it not been for his mother's insistence to take the good book, Edmonds would have lost his leg. If Edmonds was not a religious man before, he certainly was after this affair!

When the attack was over, the Union detachment lost ten men killed including Captain Reed and

Mosby Ranger John Edmonds

seven wounded. One of the wounded would later die in Vienna. Mosby claimed he captured seventy men. However, the actual number ranged from fifty to sixty. Thirty-four of the prisoners would later die in Southern prisons.

Union Major Casper Crowninshield

Mosby lost one man killed and four or five wounded. But Charlie Binns had escaped, so Mosby and his men were not happy. Great exertions were made by Mosby's men but they all failed to catch the precious prize. One of those Rangers seeking to capture Binns was Joe Richards. Ranger Richards' anxiety to capture and kill Binns was high as Binns was his stepfather who had piloted the enemy that day. When the first shot was fired however, Binns started to run and was never heard of again by the Californians or the Rangers. It is said that he stopped for one night in Winnipeg to get a bite and then went on to the North Pole!

According to his memoir on Mosby, John Scott wrote that Mosby said the next day as the prisoners was being sent to Richmond, *"Well, I have stopped a few more of you from sucking eggs!"*

Major Caspar Crowninshield, commander of the Second Massachusetts, noted in a letter that they found Reed's body stripped to shirt and drawers in the road where he fell. He also said about Reed, *"He was honest, brave, and a great friend of mine."*

41) Belmont Manor House on February 22, 1864 – 19661 Belmont Manor Lane, Ashburn (Private Property)

Belmont Historical Marker – Route 7 & Claiborne Parkway (N39°4'10" W77°29'30")

The Belmont Manor House is a five-part two-story Federal Mansion built by Ludwell Lee, son of Richard Henry Lee, between the years of 1799-1802. Notable figures such as President James Madison were often noted visitors to the plantation.

Another notable figure to enter the Belmont Manor House was Gilbert du Motier, the Marquis de Lafayette who often visited Ludwell Lee at his home. Lafayette served within the Continental Army under George Washington during the American Revolutionary War as America fought for freedom from Britain.

Belmont Manor House (N39°2'49" W77°25'58")

Around two o'clock in the morning on February 22, 1864, Captain J. Sewell Reed, Second Massachusetts Cavalry and Major Douglas Frazar, Sixteenth New York Cavalry, spent the night at the Belmont Manor House. Later that morning, Captain Reed would depart and be surprised and killed in action by Lieutenant Colonel John Singleton Mosby and his Rangers in a fight at Anker's Shop on the Leesburg and Alexandria Turnpike.

42) Guilford Station, February 22, 1864 – 21544 Old Vestals Gap Road (Vestals Gap Visitor Center), Sterling

Guilford Station Historical Marker (N39°1'9" W77°24'24")

Ranger William Chapman stopped at Guilford Station on his way to setting up an ambush site at Anker's Shop along the Leesburg and Alexandria Turnpike.

43) Shootout at Locust Grove on March 4, 1864 – 200 Locust Grove Road, Purcellville (Private Property)

Locust Grove (N39°7'42" W77°42'56")

Union Captain Samuel Means

On March 4, 1864, Union Captain "Quaker Sam" Means, with a portion of Companies A and B of the Loudoun Rangers, were scouting into Loudoun County where they learned of a detachment of the Sixth Virginia Cavalry that was near the village of Hamilton on an expedition attempting to gather new recruits. The Loudoun Rangers sent an advance guard consisting of Flemon Anderson, George Hickman, Dave Hough, and Sergeant John Forsythe of Company B, and William Bull to reconnoiter the confederates.

It was learned that the enemy was at Washington Vandevanter's home named *Locust Grove*

Mosby Ranger Gabriel V. Braden

enjoying a dance. The revelers at the dance were brothers, Hector and Gabriel V. Braden, who were having a great time at their uncle's house. Also at the dance were Isaac Vandevanter along with Clark and William H. Ball.

Upon arriving at *Locust Grove,* Means ordered two of his men to go toward the house while he and the rest of his squad remained near the barn. Loudoun Rangers William Bull and Flemon Anderson advanced to the house and entered the front door where they immediately received enemy fire from four Confederates concealed in the hall. The two Union men returned fire driving the Confederates out into the garden; where one Confederate brother, eighteen year old Hector Braden, received a bullet mortally wounding him and another bullet wounded Hector's brother Gabriel. The other two members of the Sixth Virginia Cavalry were captured by Means' Rangers. Also, one of the ladies, a Miss Braden, was slightly wounded in this encounter.

Hector would linger a few days at *Locust Grove* before he passed away. Hector's brother Gabriel was so severely shot; he was left at the house to die, but survived, and later rode with Mosby's Rangers in quite a few raids before the war ended. However, he would be hobbled with a limp for the rest of his life.

44) Ranger John deButts wounded in Leesburg on April 29, 1864 – Leesburg Courthouse Marker, 18 East Market Street, Leesburg

Loudoun County Court Square Historical Marker, Leesburg Courthouse (N39°6′56″ W77°33′52″)

On Friday, April 29, 1864, a detail of Mosby's Rangers were in Loudoun on a foraging expedition. At the same time Union Colonel Charles Russell Lowell had started from Vienna with a brigade of cavalry, supported by General Tyler's brigade of infantry from Fairfax Court House, to drive Mosby and his men out of the county and gobble them all up! A body of the Union cavalry came up to Leesburg and moved on to Middleburg where they were joined by a larger force, and together they scoured around the country for three or four days. Being so vastly superior to Mosby in numbers, the Rangers could not risk an open field fight. But by hovering around their camps, making sudden dashes, and firing on them, the Rangers kept the Union cavalry from straggling and doing more damage. Some sharp skirmishes took place at times, in which quite a number were lost on both sides.

Mosby Ranger Ewell Atwell

When the Union cavalry entered Leesburg, there were about a dozen of Mosby's men in town. A number were in and around the hotel, known as the Picket Public House, with their horses standing in the street. The Union cavalrymen were within two hundred yards of the hotel when their approach was first noticed by a group on the veranda. Rangers Ewell Atwell and Thomas J. Flack rushed to their horses, mounted, and dashed off with the enemy in hot pursuit. Flack, a genteel young man, who was sent by Mosby to haul corn from Grundell's was shot on the edge of town. Atwell, finding his pursuers gaining on him, abandoned his horse and jumping through an Osage orange hedge, made his escape. Mosby Ranger William Devine and another Ranger only identified as King ran through the hotel and out into the back yard; the former taking refuge in the house of a friend of Union sympathizers, and the latter in the Episcopal Church. Both escaped.

JOHN P. DeBUTTS, CO. A.

Mosby Ranger John deButts

All who were in the bar-room at the public house were captured except Mosby Ranger John P. deButts of Company A. He had stopped in Leesburg to have his horse shod, and being cut off from the blacksmith's shop, attempted to fight his way to his horse. He had come out of the Picket House shooting his revolver. He had unfortunately taken one drink too many and was weaving so much he made a poor target for the Yankees to shoot at. He was so drunk he hardly knew what he was about or who he even recognized. He commenced a regular duel with a Yankee upon the street. Ranger deButts, who was said to be a good shot when sober, upon this occasion he did no damage. He went for his horse, but it started plunging and rearing from all the firing going on around it, and pulled the entire Court House fence down. deButts held the Yankees off for a while until finally he went down, shot through the shoulder, and the bullet came clear on down into his elbow. He was captured and taken to Fort Delaware, Delaware, where he was kept a prisoner for eleven months and was not released until near the end of the war.

John deButts had started out as a Partisan a few months before Mosby started his first organized company. He was one of the twenty-nine who raided Fairfax Court House and captured General Stoughton. In the early part of the war, deButts served in the First Virginia Cavalry under Colonel R. Welby Carter. He was one of the thirty-five men of Company H of that regiment who made the famous charge near the Henry House at the first battle of Manassas, in which eight men were killed and the majority of the company wounded; he having his pistol shot out of his hand and finger taken with it. With Mosby, deButts displayed conspicuous gallantry at the Saint Patrick's Day Raid in Herndon in March 1863, and at Warrenton Junction a few months later. Flack was a member of Company D. His remains were taken to his home in Baltimore by his brother a few days after his death.

Arthur deButts, the grandson of Ranger John deButts still has the bullet, which was passed down through his family, that was taken from deButts when he was shot in Leesburg on April 29, 1864.

Plaque with bullet taken from Ranger John deButts. Courtesy of Grandson Arthur deButts

Bullet taken from Ranger John deButts. Courtesy of Grandson Arthur deButts

Grandson Arthur deButts with Mosby Ranger John deButts Bullet Plaque

John deButts, approximately age 70

Confederate Soldier Marker at Leesburg Courthouse (N39°6'56″ W77°33'52″)

45) Sergeant Charles B. Stewart wounded by John Mobberly on May 17, 1864 – 16125 Clark's Gap Road, Waterford or 15707 Clark's Gap Road, Waterford (Private Properties)

On Monday, May 16, 1864, Mosby Ranger Captain Dolly Richards learned that a portion of Union Captain Daniel M. Keyes Loudoun Rangers had crossed the Potomac and were in Loudoun County. Captain Richards started from Bloomfield with thirty men, hoping to have a brush with them. Richards men reached Hillsboro about ten o'clock at night and started on their trail toward Waterford, and halted before entering the village. On Tuesday morning, May 17, 1864, the Loudoun Rangers went into Waterford searching for breakfast. While the Unionists were somewhat scattered while getting something to eat, the Loudoun Rangers posted pickets on the Hamilton road. Shortly after daylight that morning, Richards with two men went into the hamlet to draw the enemy out. He was soon observed and was fired upon by six of Keyes men who then gave chase. The Loudoun Rangers followed Richards

Union Captain Daniel M. Keyes, Loudoun Rangers

into an ambush site where the majority of Richards' men were hidden and waiting for their prey. As Richards came in sight of his concealed men, he waved his hat and the Confederates commenced firing. The Loudoun Rangers were decoyed into a deadly trap that resulted in the killing of Mike Ryan and James Monegan, of Company A and dangerously wounding Sergeant Charles Stewart, of Company B.

Mosby Ranger Dolly Richards

As Richards and his partisans charged the Loudoun Rangers with a Confederate yell, Keyes' men broke and ran. Captain Keyes hurriedly led and formed his little armed force of Loudoun Rangers on a hill north of the town, where he received the onslaught of Richards and his band. Keyes and his men would fire and fall back, fighting in that manner for about three miles, while being furiously chased by Richards and his partisans. Many of the Loudoun Rangers jumped from their horses, leaving them standing while they ran and hid in the bushes. The Loudoun Rangers made a final stand about three miles outside of Waterford, but Richards did not attack again.

In that engagement, the Loudoun Rangers lost two men killed, four wounded, and had five men become prisoners; William Bull, John Ambrose, Peter Doherty, Henry Fouch, and Sergeant James H. Beatty. Richards also captured fifteen horses with their equipment. Richards and his men did not have a single man injured.

The Loudoun Rangers that were made prisoners were marched back through Waterford. A young attractive single woman, possibly Isabella "Belle" Moreland, one of the many loyal ladies of that little village, kissed Sergeant Beatty, which made the mouths of many of Mosby's men water. But it was to no avail, because the pro-Union young lass was a little particular concerning who she kissed!

Union Sergeant James H. Beatty, Loudoun Rangers

The Union prisoners were marched on through Hamilton and Upperville, in Fauquier County. That night, near Piedmont Station, Sergeant James H. Beatty made a break for liberty. He darted through the woods in the darkness like a greyhound moving fast and careful. About a hundred shots were fired after him, but he went faster than the bullets. It had been less than two months since Beatty had returned from Belle Isle Prison in Richmond, that known "Hell on Earth." The thoughts of returning so soon to that God forsaken place prompted him to outrun man and beast. He had travelled all night and part of the next day, and the next night arrived at Waterford, greatly to the delight of his friends and neighbors. He repaid his kissing lady friend with double compound interest, repaying the smooch she so ungrudgingly bestowed upon him only thirty-six hours before.

John Mobberly, a known Confederate renegade and a deserter from the Thirty-fifth Battalion Virginia Cavalry, had accompanied Richards and his men on that raid into Waterford. After the fighting had ceased, Mobberly found Sergeant Charles B. Stewart clinging to his life while lying on the ground. Stewart had been knocked from his horse in the initial volley by a bullet through his chest, and had another bullet go through his left leg, and was shot twice more by Mobberly without provocation as Stewart was defenseless to protect himself. Mobberly then rode his horse back and forth over Stewart's injured body and emptied his revolver, hitting him in the left hand and in the face shattering his jaw. Mobberly subsequently dismounted, removed Stewart's fine new Union boots, and rode off in triumph.

The notorious John W. Mobberly

16125 Clark's Gap Road, Waterford. The first potential location noted as where John Mobberly wounded Sergeant Stewart (N39°10′13″ W77°36′32″)

15707 Clark's Gap Road, Waterford. The second potential location noted as where John Mobberly wounded Sergeant Stewart (N39°10′13″ W77°36′32″)

Sergeant Stewart with four bullets through his body, was taken to Rachel Steers, a kind Quaker lady who nursed him back to life. Dr. Thomas M. Bond kindly dressed his wounds twice a day until he recovered. The venerable doctor was shocked by Mobberly's inhumane action to a man who had already surrendered and cried out, *"Surely no hell is too hot for a man that would do a thing like this."*

Stewart would survive this horrible encounter, vow to reap revenge on Mobberly, and both men would meet again under far less favorable circumstances.

The location of Sergeant Charles B. Stewart's wounding, accordion to various historians was either at 16125 Clark's Gap Road or 15707 Clark's Gap Road, a very short distance from each other.

46) Mosby skirts Berlin (Brunswick Bridge) on July 4, 1864 – Brunswick Bridge, Lovettsville

Current bridge from Virginia to Brunswick Maryland across the Potomac River (N39°18'23" W77°37'55")

About eleven o'clock in the morning on July 4, 1864, Mosby and his men reached the Potomac from Virginia where they could see the small village of Berlin across the river. The bridge that had stood there across the Potomac had been burned in June 1861 by the Confederates. Since this was not their main target, they halted a few miles downstream at a farmhouse while Mosby and a number of his men scouted the general area of Point of Rocks.

47) Mosby fires his artillery piece *Potomac* on July 4, 1864 – Point of Rocks, Route 15 and Lovettsville Road Boat Slip, Taylorstown

Point of Rocks, Route 15 & Lovettsville Road Boat Slip (N39°16'20" W77°32'49")

Later in the morning on July 4, 1864, Mosby fired his artillery piece *Potomac* at a canal boat named *Flying Cloud* which was transporting Federal Treasury employees on the Potomac towards Harper's Ferry. Mosby's artillery fire on the canal boat came from the Virginia side of the Potomac about one mile from Point of Rocks. The first shell fell short and the next two rounds went over the floating vessel causing it to run aground.

Upon the grounding, passengers jumped ashore, some taking to the hills, with others running down the railroad tracks as fast as they could run. Crew members of the ship tried to dislodge the vessel until some of Mosby's Rangers had reached the towpath. As the Rangers got close, they started firing on the ship using their revolvers forcing the crew members to flee in every direction. From their hiding places, the passengers and the crew members could see the Rangers pillaging and then burning the defenseless boat.

John Alexander noted that the Rangers seized and grabbed items such as liquor, cigars and various other items from the canal boat. Loudoun Ranger John Forsythe reported that the Rangers burned a canal boat. The Rangers then cut the telegraph lines, threw logs across the railroad tracks, hid, and waited for an unknowing Union train.

About fifteen minutes later, a train came rambling down the tracks. The engineer, seeing the smoke and steam from the burning boat, gave a whistle to stop the train very quickly, but not before the train was in range of the *Potomac*. The Confederate artillery fired four shells with one volley wounding the train's fireman in the arm. While the train was stopped, the train passengers, supposing it was captured, jumped off and were unable to get on again when the train started backing up. Some of them fell into the hands of the Rangers and were plundered of their money, hats, and anything else they wanted. However, some of the passengers on the train escaped towards the mountain.

Later that day, Mosby also fired his artillery piece *Potomac* at Companies A and B of the Loudoun Rangers and Companies G & H of the First Maryland Regiment, Potomac Home Brigade Infantry, consisting of approximately 250 Union regulars guarding Point of Rocks.

48) Mount Zion Church Fight on July 4-6, 1864 – Mount Zion Baptist Church – 40309 John Mosby Highway, Aldie

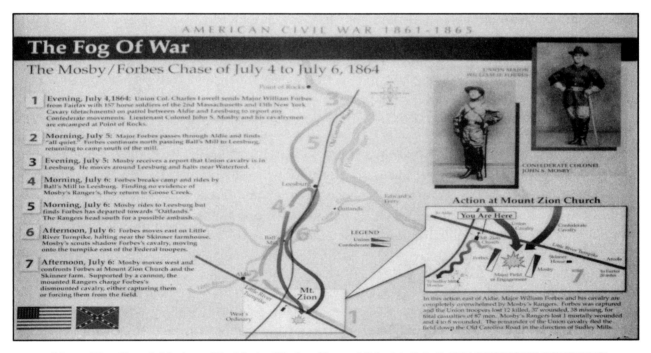

Mount Zion Church Marker – The Mosby / Forbes Chase of July 4 to July 6, 1864 (N38°57'49" W77°36'44")

After crossing the Potomac at Point of Rocks late on July 4, 1864, leaving Maryland, Mosby headed to Waterford where he halted and threw up pickets on the Leesburg road on July 5, 1864. After spending the night, Mosby dispatched David Grafton Carlisle and John Puryear to Leesburg at daylight on July 6. They soon returned and reported that Major William H. Forbes of Boston was in town. Forbes with his crack California Battalion, together with elements of the Thirteenth New York Cavalry, had come up from Fairfax the evening before and was in that neighborhood looking for and seeking an encounter with Mosby hoping they would run across him. His commander, Colonel Charles R. Lowell, was heard to call Forbes, "His fighting Major."

Mosby Ranger David G. Carlisle

Union Major William H. Forbes

The Rangers presence in the immediate vicinity must have been known to the many Union sympathizers there, for some of the Rangers had gone to Leesburg the night after the attack on Point of Rocks to lay their trophies at the feet of their lady-loves. Indeed, the firing on the river at Point of Rocks, which had been kept up with more or less regularity throughout that day proclaimed that things were going on in which the Second Massachusetts Cavalry with additional troopers from New York might participate if they had a hankering for a fight. It is incredible that Forbes did not know that the Rangers were only a few miles away. Mosby and his men were giving their undivided attention to the Unionist Loudoun Rangers and Forbes could have attacked their rear and caused Mosby all kinds of serious problems if had he decided to do so.

Upon receiving the report of the scouts, Colonel Mosby ordered the Rangers up and started out in pursuit of Major Forbes who was singing cheerfully as they rode along towards Leesburg. But that gentleman seemed still inclined to elude glory; for when the Rangers passed Fort Johnston a mile from town, they saw the Union cavalrymen moving out in the direction of Aldie. There were about one hundred and fifty of them, finely mounted and equipped, and they had the reputation of being good fighters and well disciplined. Mosby's men had been reduced to less than two hundred by the departure of some of the Rangers to their families and safe houses in the Leesburg area. The Rangers also knew that bringing on a fight with Forbes was not going to be a picnic.

But when the Rangers reached Leesburg around nine o'clock that morning, they found out about the high boasts of how anxious Forbes and his men were to meet them in battle, and how they were going to annihilate Mosby's partisans if they actually met them eye to eye. These taunts were communicated to the entire command by the pretty girls of Leesburg who lined the streets as the Rangers passed through the town offering them food for their breakfast. That was the first visit to that ancient town for Ranger John Alexander which possibly made a pleasant impression upon him because he made it his home after the war, and he continued to live there until he died in 1909. The Southern women, as well as the provisions and the Union boasts, put the Rangers in a very nasty fighting mood and they did not linger as they went after those Californians with a renewed determination to wipe them off the face of the earth.

Colonel Mosby, however, was a wily as well as a daring fighter who never let his valor get the better of his discretion, at least not in the handling of his men. He always sought to secure for them every possible advantage for a fight, and his almost unvarying success in these combat encounters was one of the marks of his genius. The loss of one of his trained partisans was a much more serious matter to him than the loss of any Yankees was to their side, and he could not afford to play a swapping game.

Mosby learned that Forbes was striking for Mount Zion, the old church on the Little River Turnpike about two miles east of Aldie and some ten miles south of Leesburg. He assumed that they would take the most direct route there on the road which crosses Goose Creek at Ball's Mill. The natural advantages there for a surprise party were exceptional so after making a hurried detour, the Rangers arrived there first and got into position to receive Forbes and his cavalrymen.

The Rangers mounted men were formed for a charge behind the bluff around which the road winds after crossing the creek, while dismounted sharpshooters were hidden among the bushes along its crest facing the enemy if they should cross the broad creek bottoms and enter the ford. The carbines were to open on the Union cavalry as they crossed the creek, and while they were thereby disconcerted, the mounted Rangers would charge them. Unfortunately, the Rangers waited there for some time before it became known that the enemy had gone to Mount Zion by another road. The partisans then moved from there by an obscure road which came out on the pike about two miles east of Mount Zion before halting.

Mount Zion Church (N38°57'49" W77°36'44")

Believed to be Mosby Ranger John Waller

Colonel Mosby vigorously scouted the area and when he arrived back, he joined with John Munson, John Waller, Willie Mosby, Wat Bowie, Bushrod Underwood, and a few others riding cross country. The other Rangers noticed that Mosby had changed horses and now was mounted on his favorite sorrel mare. Whenever Mosby appeared mounted on her, the Rangers knew

Mosby Ranger Walter "Wat" Bowie

implicitly there was serious business to be soon taken care of.

Mosby Ranger Bushrod Underwood

Mosby had located Forbes in a field just south of the pike in which they had halted to feed. To the west of them was a large brick dwelling and grounds. East of them, leaving the field and crossing the turnpike, was a body of woods about a hundred yards wide. The woods hid the Yankees from the Rangers view when Mosby and his men came out on the pike on top of a hill nearly a mile below them. Their pickets in the woods doubtless discovered Mosby at once. So this was not to be a case of surprise, but a straight charge over an open road upon an enemy who was fully prepared for them. The only advantage of their position was that the Rangers were between them and their home in Fairfax. This was certain to make Forbes and his cavalrymen fight all the more desperately.

About a dozen Ranger carbineers under Lieutenant Harry Hatcher were ordered toward the Union troops in a sweeping gallop and quickly dismounted and tore a gap in the fence at the corner of the field. While this was occurring, Mosby's artillery piece, the twelve pounder howitzer *Potomac* supported by Lieutenant Alfred Glascock's men, was being placed in position on the hill as the mounted Rangers formed for the charge to be led by Mosby himself.

Mosby ordered the Rangers to hold their fire until he could get into the field and went along the pike rather leisurely, not giving their horses full rein until they got through the newly opened gap in the fence. The enemy's pickets in the woods fired some ineffectual shots at the sharpshooters, but when Mosby finally charged and got within a hundred yards of the pickets they broke and ran back upon the main body with Forbes. When the Rangers galloped into the woods which the Union pickets had vacated, and scattered along the edge next to them, Forbes and his men were now totally in sight.

A couple of hundred yards in front of the mounted partisans upon the slope of the hill in the old field, the Californians and New Yorkers were drawn up into two lines, one behind the other, facing the Rangers. Their alignment was as perfect as if on dress parade. The Union officers were in position with their sabres drawn, and their men sat on their horses with carbines ready. The shots which the partisans fired at them from the woods seemed to be returned with absolute regularity at intervals along their line. The enemy was armed with Spencer seven shooters, pistols, and sabres while the Rangers had nothing but revolvers.

The Rangers came whooping up the pike. Just before the Rangers reached the front line of the Union cavalry Mosby's howitzer boomed and sent a shell over their heads. The blue line seemed to break and waiver from the single artillery round just as the head of Mosby's attacking force swept past the sharpshooters. It was at the torn fence where Lieutenant Albert Wrenn, with a section of Company B, dashed through it and up the hill to join the battle. The attack struck the Yankees while they were attempting to reform when the first Ranger column was upon them. Major Forbes occupied the center of the action, standing in his stirrups with sabre drawn, fighting desperately.

Mosby Ranger Lieutenant Albert Wrenn

Ranger J. Marshall Crawford wrote after the war, *"Major Forbes, the bravest Federal officer we ever met, tried to rally his men in the field on the right of the road, three times failing in his efforts. His last effort was a beautiful retreat behind a fence which stretched across the field. Drawing his sabre, he cried, 'Rally around your major for the last time, and repulse them."*

It was here that Mosby would have been cut in two by Forbes' sabre, but for the brave Tom Richards, who warded off the blow with his pistol and received a severe flesh wound in the shoulder from Forbes sabre thrust. Richards snapped his pistol in the major's face, but it failed to explode. In that instant, a bullet ripped into Forbes' horse, and he went down under the dying animal pinning him helplessly. Forbes, seeing no chance of escape, surrendered like a brave soldier to Richards. Lieutenant Amory, also a prominent citizen of Boston, fell side by side with his commander.

Union Chaplain Charles A. Humphreys described the fighting as such, *"Mosby and his Rangers were upon us, swooping down like Indians, yelling like fiends, discharging their pistols with fearful rapidity, and threatening to completely envelop our little band. Who could stand before such a charge?"* Obviously, the members of Forbes command were unable to withstand this type of attack.

While Forbes was fighting, the Rangers on the fleetest horses had gotten up to the Union cavalrymen both in their front and on their flank. Some of the Union cavalrymen took on the Rangers toe-to-toe and fought gallantly. The Rangers closed in on them and also fought hand-to-hand. The Union saddles were quickly being emptied by the deadly revolvers in the hands of the experienced Rangers who knew no tactics except for the ability to fight hard at all times. It was a mass of struggling, cursing maniacs, each striving to slay his antagonist.

Union Chaplain Charles A. Humphreys

Union Captain Goodwin Stone

Some of these same Second Massachusetts Cavalrymen were the men the Rangers had met previously at Dranesville on February 22, 1864. The fighting was so intense by everyone that the Union line soon waivered and broke with Union cavalrymen running as fast as they could in every direction. Union Chaplain Charles A. Humphreys stated that Captain Goodwin Stone, displayed great coolness and for a moment succeeded in holding a handful of his men together, who poured one volley into the ranks of the Confederate pursuers, but that Stone himself received a bullet wound and fell forward upon his horse's neck. It was a fatal wound, as the ball lodged in his spine. But though he was partially paralyzed, he had strength enough left to hold on, and for a few moments he galloped along with chaplain Humphreys. The guerillas were sharply pursuing Stone, and he was conscious that he could do no more in the way of rallying his men, and took the first opportunity to escape running into the wooded area. The full Union rout was now on. Ranger John Alexander's horse Joe was unaccountably slow and lifeless during that engagement in spite of his most vigorous spurring in trying to join the fight.

Humphreys, who would be captured the next day by Mosby's men found out later that Stone's faithful steed carried him—helpless as he was—fourteen miles towards camp, and he was, the next day, picked up by a Union ambulance and taken to a Union hospital in Falls Church, where, though every attention was given to him, he died on July 18, 1864. His last words to Humphreys were *"Save yourself, Chaplain."*

All the way across the fields the fighting and capturing had been kept up so that when the Sudley road was reached most the enemy had been shot or captured. There were very few of them who rode out on that highway that afternoon. When Alexander reached Corner Hall, about two miles south of the church, he met the last of the Rangers coming back who informed him that not more than five or six of the enemy had gotten away, and that Colonel Mosby and young Johnnie Edmonds were after them. They, too, soon returned with the report that the fugitives had cleanly outridden them. Dead and wounded men and horses were lying all along the road and the fields. Munson found a man kneeling near the fence by the roadside, with his head bent forward touching the ground in front of him and his left hand clutching a gaping wound in his side. Munson was ordered to go to his assistance, but when he dismounted and tried to raise him or ease his position, all he found was a dead corpse.

The fighting and the rout lasted until late in the afternoon, and there were so many wounded men to help, and so many prisoners to look after, that the Rangers did not start homeward bound until long after dark.

This was a proud day for Mosby. He had vanquished, in fact annihilated Forbes' command, who had been out three days looking for him. Mosby with around one hundred and seventy-five fighting men, had earned a well-deserved victory which was by no means a bloodless one. Eight of the Rangers were wounded; five of whom, Henry Smallwood, Hugh Waters, Bob Walker, Tom Lake, and Frank Woolf felt the pain of a Yankee bullet. Smallwood's death, which soon followed the next day, was a great sorrow to Mosby's command. He was a quiet, unostentatious little fellow, and absolutely reliable. The others recovered and survived the war---through a special Providence.

Lieutenant Colonel John S. Mosby

Another Ranger, young Willie Martin, was so closely surrounded by Forbes' men that they clubbed him insensible using their Union carbines as a battering rod. Martin ended up badly bruised and sore from these violent collisions. However, this did not stop Martin even after having his horse shot from under him early in the action, from pursuing an enemy combatant on foot, and at dark returning to camp, mounted on a fine Union horse with one Union prisoner as his prize.

109

Mount Zion Church Marker – The Mosby-Forbes Engagement July 6, 1864

Night fell before the Rangers gathered themselves together. The nearby mansion house was turned into a hospital, and the occupants, the family of Samuel Skinner, were indefatigable in their ministrations to the wounded. It was necessary for the partisans to remain there for some hours and pickets were posted.

Ranger Alexander was posted in the road below the house and on the edge of the battlefield. It was not a good night for Alexander while on picket duty. The groans of the wounded men and horses, the pitiful calls for relief, the prayers, and the heart-rending laments for loved ones were borne to him on the quiet summer night from the most distant parts of the field. To hear a poor fellow, within a few rods perhaps, calling for water, or for someone to move his dead horse off his broken leg, or to raise his head and let him die in peace, and yet not dare to leave his sentry post and go toward them was an awful trial to a boy of warm sympathies. As Alexander sat on his horse that night and listened to these sounds and thought of his young friends perhaps dying, up at the house, he realized what a modern soldier had so aptly formulated into the words, "War is Hell!"

There was another incident that occurred during that fight which may deem trivial to the reader, but had to be documented by Alexander. After Alexander and the Rangers finally halted for the night in a grassy field some miles up the road near Middleburg, the horses were turned loose to graze on the luxuriant clover. Alexander laid on the soft ground and used his saddle as a pillow. When he awoke in the early morning light, he saw his horse standing at his feet with his head bending over him. His breast and forelegs were covered with clotted blood which had flowed from an ugly bullet wound. How long he stood there in mute silence for sympathy and relief, Alexander did not know, perhaps all night. But Alexander soon realized how cruelly he had spurred him in the chase the evening before. How without a groan of protest, Joe had responded the best he could, and how patiently he had stood with him; all unconscious of the steed's suffering, on that lonely miserable watch. Alexander was not ashamed to throw his arms around his horse's neck and weep out his grief and contrition. Poor Joe, that was Alexander's last ride in battle together.

Mosby was not unmindful of Tom Richards endangering his own life to save him. Mosby recommended to the Secretary of War in Richmond that Richards be sent to the Northern Neck to break up the blockade-running carried on in that quarter. Richards would win the appointment, gain promotion to captain, be given command of men, and rendered good service in that area.

Although Tom Richards did his best to kill the Union commanding officer in that fight, he captured him alive and Major Forbes would survive the war. Major William H. Forbes returned to Massachusetts after the war, and up to the time of his death, was one of the most influential, beloved, and respected citizens in that commonwealth. Munson contacted him after the war in his Boston office, and they fought the war over again with all the zest at their command. In the course of their conversation, Forbes put his hand on Munson's knee and said, *"Tell me, Munson, how is my old friend, Tom Richards?"* John Munson wrote after hearing that statement from Forbes, *"Surely to recall Tom Richards as his friend was enough to convince any listener that the North and the South are again united."*

Union Captain William H. Forbes

Mosby reported afterwards *"....meeting them (Forbes) at Mount Zion Church, and completely routing them, with a loss of about eighty of their officers and men left dead and severely wounded on the field, besides fifty-seven prisoners. Their loss includes a captain and lieutenant killed and one lieutenant severely wounded, the major commanding and two lieutenants prisoners. We have also secured all their horses, arms, etc."*

Mosby further stated his *"...loss was one killed and six wounded—none dangerously. The next day the booty was divided at Piedmont, and the prisoners sent to Richmond. Thus terminated one of Mosby's most brilliant victories! After this raid the enemy never ventured, in two months after, the experiment of another raid through that portion of our district."*

Mount Zion Church Marker

49) Mosby dines at *Temple Hall* on July 5, 1864 – 15829 Temple Hall Lane, Leesburg (Private Property)

Temple Hall (N39°10′29″ W77°31′42″)

Late in the afternoon, on July 5, 1864, John S. Mosby stopped at *Temple Hall* to take supper at the house of Henry Ball, a well-known individual in the Leesburg area. While Mosby was enjoying his repast Rangers John Thomas and Harry Hatcher returned from a scout with the information that two hundred Union cavalry were at Leesburg looking and searching for Mosby and his Rangers. It was at this point that Mosby gave the order to move his men towards Waterford leading to the fight at Mount Zion Church on July 6.

50) Yankee Davis House – .2 miles west of Mount Zion Church on John Mosby Highway, Aldie (Private Property)

Very near Mount Zion Church in a grove of trees on the right side of the road going towards Aldie formerly stood the home of Alexander G. "Yankee" Davis, a Union sympathizer and scout for the Union Army. Yankee Davis would survive the war and continued to live in the neighborhood after the war. Partly, because he was an excellent shot and the ex-confederates knew he would retaliate against any kind of transgression against his property or family.

Location of Yankee Davis House in the clump of trees in the background (N38°57'58" W77°36'53")

Remains at location of Yankee Davis house (N38°57'58" W77°36'53")

Alexander G. "Yankee" Davis

51) Samuel Skinner House, after Mount Zion Church Fight – 40513 John Mosby Highway, Aldie (Private Property)

Wounded Confederate soldiers were cared for at the Samuel Skinner House (N38°57'41" W77°36'07")

The Skinner house was turned into a Confederate hospital after the fighting ceased at Mount Zion Church.

52) Lenah Farm Lane – 20413 John Mosby Highway & Lenah Farm Road, Aldie

The road Mosby reportedly took from Ball's Mill towards the Little River Turnpike on his way to Mount Zion Church on July 6, 1864 (N38°57'11" W77°34'47")

53) Mosby attacks Union wagon train in Snickersville on July 20, 1864 – Snickersville

On July 20, 1864, Mosby, with Companies A & D, moved through Loudoun County getting in the rear of the Union forces in the area. On coming around near Snickersville, a large Union wagon train was seen in camp with a heavy cavalry guard.

Mosby made several unsuccessful attempts to draw out a portion of the guard. A few of Mosby's men would ride out in full view of the camp and after showing themselves, retreated. Then they would ride closer and fire on the guards.

Finding all efforts to entice them away from the train fruitless, Mosby started off, saying he would go back and bring on the remainder of the command and attack the wagon train again. Mosby, however, would not go back.

54) Fight against the Eighth New York Cavalry at Mount Airy on September 15, 1864 – 232 Harry Byrd Highway, Bluemont

Union General George H. Chapman and Staff

On September 15, 1864, Union General George H. Chapman with the Eighth New York Cavalry crossed the Shenandoah River at Castleman's Ferry. General Chapman then proceeded to ride into Loudoun County seeking Mosby and his notorious band.

After going to Paris, General Chapman returned through Upperville to Snickersville where he paused to rest his command. A detachment commanded by Captain James Bliss was sent to the top of the mountain to keep watch and to meet with an element of the Eighth New York Cavalry, led by Captain Hartwell Compson, which had been detached after crossing the river with orders to scout along the banks further up-river.

Ranger Captain William Chapman with forty Mosby Rangers had been alerted to the movements of the Eighth New York Cavalry and cautiously followed them along the mountain to the gap. Seeing that the Union company was lounging about and were unprepared for any kind of enemy activity, Captain Chapman immediately attacked scattering the Union troopers in every direction.

Captain Chapman was able to capture eighteen Union prisoners, forty horses and release some twelve Confederate prisoners who had been captured earlier. Captain Chapman and his Rangers were long gone before the main Union force at Snickersville could come to the assistance of their surprised comrades. Captain Chapman lost Joseph Johnson as the only Ranger killed, suffered three Rangers wounded, and had four men captured; Rangers Robert Hooe, John A. Marchant, Francis Darden, and Benton V. Fletcher. The *Washington Star* called Darden and Hooe "renegade Washingtonians." All the Rangers were committed to a military prison.

Mount Airy Fight Marker (N39°6′57″ W77°50′47″)

55) Mosby divides money after Greenback Raid on October 15, 1864 – Ebenezer Church, 20427 Airmont Road, Bluemont

Between two and three o'clock, October 14, 1864, Mosby with eighty men derailed a train outside of Harper's Ferry and captured two paymasters with a tin box and a satchel. When the U.S. dollars, called greenbacks, in the tin box and the satchel were added together, they amounted to the handsome sum of one hundred and seventy-three thousand dollars.

Ebenezer Churches – Built in 1755 and 1855 (N39°8′27″ W77°48′41″)

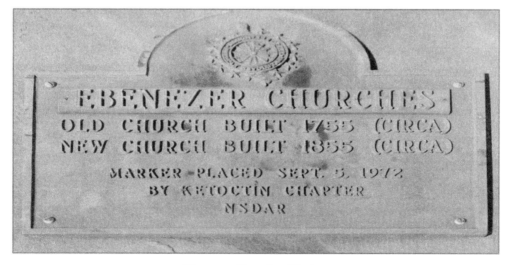

Ebenezer Churches Marker

Mosby confiscated the greenbacks and after meeting the next day, the 15th, at the Ebenezer Churches, he ordered Fount Beattie, Charley Hall, Charlie Grogan, and Daniel Briscoe to count and divide all the greenbacks among the boys who were on that raid, so that each one received about $2,200 in crisp new greenbacks, in uncut sheets of various denominations. Every Ranger involved in that raid would leave with a full haversack of U.S. Government equity!

56) Mosby purchases his horse "Coquette" at Oatlands Plantation, October 1864 – 20850 Oatlands Plantation Lane, Leesburg

At Ebenezer Church, in Loudoun County after the Greenback Raid on October 14, 1864, Mosby divided up $173,000 for eight-four Rangers with each receiving approximately $2,200 (give or take a hundred dollars or two). Mosby's train wreckers made a very nice haul.

The Rangers were extremely thankful for the greenbacks that they tried to give a share to Mosby. Mosby however, would have none of it. He never accepted any of the spoils from his raids. Mosby's men attempted to give a nice monetary amount to Mrs. Mosby of $8,000 to $10,000, but the colonel found out about it and gave it back. He is quoted as saying, *"Boys I didn't go into Confederate service for money or plunder....We don't want the money you saw proper to present to Mrs. Mosby and I'm going to hand it back and divide it amongst you."*

Mosby's men were determined to do something special for their commander, so they collected a purse and bought him a beautiful thoroughbred horse he had previously spotted at *Oatlands* Farm and presented it to him as a gift. Mosby accepted the horse. It was the only offering Mosby ever accepted from his men that came from the captured booty from a raid.

Front of *Oatlands* House (N39°2′47″ W77°37′15″)

Rear of *Oatlands* House

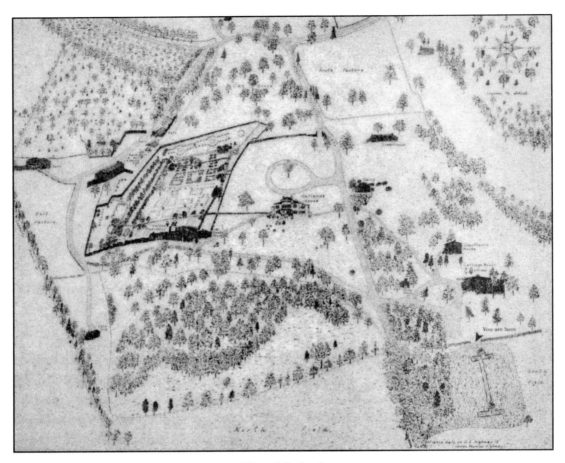

Map of *Oatlands*

South Pasture at *Oatlands*

122

OATLANDS
★ ★ ★
Civil War Comes to Oatlands

The Civil War arrived in Loudoun County on October 21, 1861, with the Battle of Ball's Bluff. As Confederate forces gathered to protect Leesburg, Elizabeth Grayson Carter, the widowed mistress of Oatlands, wrote in her journal on October 17, *"Our troops falling back on Centreville—Mississippi Regt's. encamped at the Mill —Soldiers here all day."*

Elizabeth's son Benjamin served with the 8th Virginia Infantry Regiment, while her son George acted as a courier. On the day of the battle, she wrote, *"A day of excitement—Ben came home at night wounded in the little finger. Wonderful escape—Terrible Battle near Leesburg— great victory for us tho' our loss is great."*

Anticipating another Union attack, Confederate Gen. Nathan "Shanks" Evans withdrew his exhausted troops to Carter's Mill on Goose Creek and told Mrs. Carter he intended to make Oatlands his headquarters. Before leaving for the safety of her family home in Upperville on October 23, she wrote: *"Servants cooked all day for this last detachment of prisoners. 131 prisoners passed. We left O[atlands] for Bellefield. Troops collecting in field beyond the creek. 2 new Regiments and part of the Washington Artillery arrived. General Evans and Staff made O. Headquarters."*

Elizabeth Carter remained at her Upperville residence until her death in 1885. Oatlands served throughout the war as a haven for family, friends, and soldiers, including Eppa Hunton, Norborne Berkeley, Baron Von Massow, and Mosby's Rangers.

***Oatlands* Civil War Marker**

Rangers on Horseback

Coquette would become Mosby's favorite fighting horse.

57) Ranger Richard Montjoy killed at Goresville on November 27, 1864 – 14880 James Monroe Highway & Spinks Ferry Road, Lucketts

Loudoun Ranger Joseph T. Ritchie

On November 26, 1864, Captain Richard P. Montjoy, with Company D, went down into the lower part of Loudoun County in search of the Loudoun Rangers. Not finding them at Waterford, one of their favorite resorts, Montjoy and Lieutenant Charlie Grogan proceeded in the direction of Leesburg.

Lieutenants Robert Graham and Augustus Rhodes, with thirty-nine Loudoun Rangers crossed the Potomac late in the evening and marched until about two o'clock the next morning. They rested six hours until eight o'clock, on November 27th before continuing their search for a large force of Mosby Rangers. The Loudoun Rangers advanced towards Leesburg, which was found to be occupied by a detachment of Mosby's men. Lieutenant Rhodes led a charge into town by the Winchester pike and the Rangers approached Mosby's men who had concealed themselves in the town. Two of

Mosby Ranger R. P. Montjoy

Mosby's Rangers mounted on fine horses, endeavored to escape by going out the pike east of town. Loudoun Rangers Sergeant Ed T. White, John S. Densmore, Joseph T. Ritchie, and Mahlon H. Best gave chase. Colonel Cleveland Coleman of the Fifth Virginia Cavalry was soon overtaken. The other officer, riding a long, gaunt roan horse, bid farewell for his escape.

However, while crossing the railroad his horse fell pinning the rider to the ground. As the Loudoun Rangers rode up, the officer cried out: *"Gentleman, won't you please get this horse off of my leg?"* Densmore, Ritchie, White, and Best dismounted, and soon extricated Captain Frederick Waugh Smith, the Assistant Adjutant General, of General Jubal Early's staff. He was a son of ex-

Loudoun Ranger Mahlon H. Best

Governor "Extra Billy" Smith. The Loudoun Rangers made a brief acquaintance which was exceptionally pleasant. As the Loudoun Rangers took the prisoners back through Leesburg, some young ladies presented them with several friendly greenbacks to "cheer them on the way." Lieutenants Graham and Rhodes of the Loudoun Rangers marched their men for camp, going out towards the Point of Rocks road.

Loudoun Ranger John Densmore

As the head of the column approached Goresville near Paxton's Store, about fifty yards in their front, in a slight hollow on the Point of Rocks road, Company D of Mosby's Rangers was formed in line of battle was. They raised a yell and the firing began. Mosby's Rangers soon repatriated the Confederate prisoners and captured several surprised Loudoun Rangers in this desperate hand to hand running fight.

Captain Frederick Waugh Smith

Site where Montjoy was killed (N39°12'19" W77°32'12")

The Loudoun Rangers who were near enough in front to go out the Taylorstown road were all quickly captured, except for Sam Fry, who rode a buckskin and raced in another direction. Those that were further in the rear escaped, with perhaps one or two exceptions. Sergeants James H. Beatty, M. S. Gregg, privates Mahlon H. Best, Henry Cole with others went out through the Whipmore farm and were closely pressed by Mosby's men, led by Captain Richard Montjoy himself. This force had soon captured M. S. Gregg and was in close pursuit of the others. Briscoe Goodhart, a Loudoun Ranger wrote, *"M. H. Best turned in his saddle, took deliberate aim, fired, and killed Montjoy, the ball entering his brain."*

Mosby Ranger John Munson's account stated, *"Montjoy....was close on his heels when the man threw his six-shooter over his shoulder, pointed it backwards without aim and pulled the trigger. The bullet went straight into Montjoy's head. Every man of his company who witnessed the tragedy reined in his horse involuntarily and groaned. We never filled Montjoy's place. We never tried to. There was only one Captain Montjoy."*

This ended the contest for the day. In the confusion that followed, M.S. Gregg escaped. The Loudoun Rangers lost as prisoners Lieutenants Rhodes and Graham, John M. Davis. Webb Franklin, P. H. Heater, Peter Fry, John Lambert; and had four Loudoun Rangers wounded, Graham, John W. Lenhart, Peter Fry, and Jacob Cordell. The latter was not captured. Mosby lost one killed, Captain Montjoy with four other of his Rangers wounded.

A few days later Colonel Mosby issued the following eloquent but sad notice to his grieving command:

General Orders-----   *Headquarters 43d Battalion P. R.*

December 3, 1864

Partisan Rangers:

The Lieutenant-Colonel Commanding announces to the battalion, with emotions of deep sorrow, the death of Captain R. P. Montjoy, who fell in action near Leesburg on the twenty-seventh ultimo, a costly sacrifice to victory. He died too early for liberty and his country's cause, but not too early for his own fame. To his Comrades in arms he has bequeathed an immortal example of daring and valor, and to his country a name that will brighten the pages of her history.

John S. Mosby,

Lieutenant-Colonel, Commanding

58) Results of the Union burning raid from November 28 through December 2, 1864 at Potts Mill – Intersection of Woodgrove and Stoney Point Roads, near Hillsboro

Potts Mill (N39°11'41" W77°44'54")

On November 28, 1864, two brigades of Union cavalry under General Wesley Merritt had crossed the Shenandoah River at Berry's Ferry and advanced through Ashby's Gap. They had come over for the purpose of laying waste to Mosby's Confederacy. Many of the Union troopers armed only with a torch, that terrible implement of war, went from one place to another using it whenever possible. As an excuse for his savage and barbarous proceeding, they claimed to do so with the object of driving Mosby from the country. Mosby, however, remained and was among those least affected by the burning.

That night the Union forces camped near Upperville, while all around them the fires blazed on. As the night wind stirred up the dying embers of the result of some poor farmer's toil, the bright flames would shoot up for a few moments, illuminating the scene and then again relapsing into darkness.

Early on the morning of November 29th, the Rangers arose hoping to find the enemy after their devastating acts of the previous day. But it was a vain hope---the Rangers found the Union army's work of destruction had only commenced. Another brigade of Union cavalry crossed the Shenandoah and marched through Snicker's Gap to join the force of military incendiaries. Soon the curling smoke was rising in dense volumes, streaming heavenward, as if appealing to God for mercy. As the fires became more numerous, the heavy mass of smoke spread out and settled over the Valley like a thick fog, obscuring the view so thoroughly that the Rangers could not see one another if they were beyond ten yards from each other.

The Union cavalry separated into three parties, one of which went along the Bloomfield road and down Loudoun in the direction of the Potomac; another passed along the Piedmont pike to Rectortown, Salem (today's Marshall) and around to Middleburg; while the main body kept along the turnpike to Aldie, where they struck the Snickersville pike. Thus, they scoured the country completely from the Blue Ridge to the Bull Run Mountains.

From the afternoon of November 28th until Friday morning December 2nd, they ranged through the beautiful Valley of Loudoun and a portion of Fauquier County, burning and destroying all in their path. They robbed the people of everything they could destroy or carry off---horses, cows, cattle, sheep, hogs, and anything else they could handle. Killing poultry, insulting women, pillaging houses, and in many cases robbing even the poor Negroes. They burned all the mills and factories as well as hay, wheat, corn, straw, and every description of forage. Barns and stables, whether full or empty, were burned. When the hogs had been killed by the farmers and hung up to cool off, the Union ruffians would take an axe, chop the hams off, and drop the remainder in the mud.

At the widow Fletcher's place, where the hogs had been killed for her winter's supply of meat, the soldiers made a pile of rails upon which the hogs were placed and burned. This was all the meat that the poor woman had to feed her children with the ensuing winter coming on. They even went to the Poor House and burned and destroyed the supplies provided for the helpless and dependent paupers. On various previous occasions, however, the Alms House had been visited by Union raiding parties where there was very little left. The Union troopers applied the torch to everything except the houses. In some portions of Loudoun, Quakers and Union sympathizers were spared, but the Southern population did not escape the immense smoke and flame arising from the smoldering ruins as far as the eye could see.

Colonel Mosby did not call the command together. Therefore there was no organized resistance, but Rangers managed to save a great deal of livestock for the farmers by driving them off to places of safety. In many instances, after the first day of the burning, the Rangers would run off stock from the path of the raiders into the limits of the district already torched, where they would hide them in a desolate location where they could not be seen. The Rangers also annoyed the Union burners in small squads and suddenly dashing in among them whenever an opportunity offered, shooting on all sides and then scampering off. In this way, a number of Union men were killed and wounded.

Welt Hatcher, seeing a Union officer riding along in the midst of his men, charged him with his revolver blazing, mortally wounding him. The Union officer's men pressed a carriage into service and took him to the Pot House where he died. After the shooting, Hatcher escaped uninjured although fired upon from all sides.

Merritt's men also captured many individuals that they believed to be Mosby's men. These individuals were brought before the provost marshal at Snickersville. The prisoners all denied that they were Mosby's men except for one man. This insolent individual was Newton Jackson. As he was carried before the seat of military justice, it was whispered among the other prisoners that he truly was a Mosby Ranger. But Mr. Burwell, of Millwood, replied, *"No, he is too badly dressed and is too much of a rough to belong to the Partisan Battalion."*

When Jackson was questioned on that point, he boldly acknowledged that he belonged with Mosby. He was threatened with hanging, but in the spirit of haughty defiance the prisoner proudly told the provost that he dared not execute his threat, for Mosby was provided with the means of retaliation. After hearing Jackson's defiant statements, Mr. Burwell remarked, *"I was mistaken. This is one of Mosby's men."*

The next day about two o'clock in the morning, the Union camp was alarmed by the startled cry of *"Mosby!"* But nothing was found disturbed except for a stampede of the cattle that also possessed a big white bull that was now no longer on the premises. That bull had been previously confiscated by Union authorities from the local populous and was known by all in the neighborhood as "Carter's Bull." However, it was soon discovered that the impudent guerilla Newton Jackson had also disappeared. The next morning, the provost instituted an investigation about the disturbance of the cattle and the disappearance of Jackson. When Burwell was called upon, he testified that when he saw Jackson last, he was mounted on Carter's white bull making his way to Number Six (today's Rokeby Road). Newton Jackson would never be seen from again!

59) Results of the Union burning raid from November 28 through December 2, 1864 at Sally's Mill – 23667 Sally's Mill Road, Middleburg (Private Property)

Sally's Mill between Aldie and Middleburg (N38°57′53″ W77°41′29″)

60) Results of the Union burning raid from November 28 through December 2, 1864 at White Pump Marker – 19397 Colchester Road, Purcellville

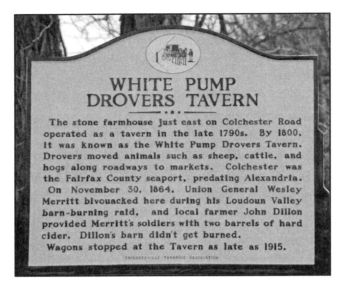

White Pump Marker (N39°4′21″ W77°45′13″)

61) Results of the Union burning raid from November 28 through December 2, 1864 at White Pump Tavern – Snickersville Turnpike & Colchester Road, Purcellville (Private Property)

White Pump Tavern, spared from the Union burning raid (N39°4′21″ W77°45′20″)

Owner John Dillard gave Union General Wesley Merritt's men two barrels of hard cider which saved his house during the burning raid.

62) Union deserter "French Bill" Loge captured on November 30, 1864 in Lovettsville

The Union sympathizing citizens in the German settlement of Lovettsville had been greatly annoyed by the various Confederate raids of Colonel Mosby's and Colonel Elijah White's cavalrymen seeking forage and supplies throughout the war. They especially thought they were being tormented by the daily excursions of John Mobberly and his favorite henchman known only by the alias of "French Bill."

Mobberly's band generally had two to fifteen men and would disappear into the Short Hills whenever Union cavalry would appear. Due to the deprivations created by Mobberly, the Union authorities at Harper's Ferry tried various plans to break-up this band. Finally, this matter was placed in the hands of the Loudoun Rangers led by Corporal S.E. Tritapoe, Joseph T. Ritchie, Joseph Fry, and Wilson Lathen who were ordered to Virginia on November 30, 1864 to try and capture some or all of Mobberly's gang.

Tritapoe immediately learned that a patrol of Mobberly's guerillas was near Lovettsville. By the aid of a light snow and newly made horse tracks, the Loudoun Rangers were able to trace them to the residence and stillhouse of Charles Johnson, a Union man, where one of the Confederates was quickly surrounded presumably after partaking of the liquid at the stillhouse. This Confederate was full of fight and began shooting at his uninvited visitors. Finally, Tritapoe and Ritchie charged the man, clubbing the revolver out of his hand and making him their prisoner. This Confederate soldier was none other than the notorious killer and assassin "French Bill."

"French Bill," or Emile Loge, had deserted both the Sixtieth and the Fifty-third New York Infantry. He was a professional bounty jumper in addition to his other serious charges. French Bill became a companion of John Mobberly's guerillas and had captured the surgeon of the Sixth Pennsylvania Cavalry and brutally murdered him. Upon his capture, French Bill was taken to the nearby Point of Rocks and turned over to Captain D. Henry Barnete, provost marshal, who had him taken to Harper's Ferry and placed in the custody of General John D. Stevenson.

On December 1, 1864, Captain Bartnete wrote a letter to General Stevenson stating: *"French Bill, of Moberly's {Mobberly's} freebooters, was captured yesterday by Keye's men........If so, he is an important capture, as he is a deserter.....I will bring him to Harper's Ferry."* In another letter dated that same day, General Stevenson wrote to Major General Philip Sheridan saying, *"I caught French Bill yesterday, a notorious murderer and bushwhacker, belonging to White's battalion, who was with the party that murdered the surgeon......."* Sheridan replied that same day stating, *"As soon as you can have fully ascertained that you have French Bill as your prisoner, take him out and hang him. This will be your authority."* Stevenson responded again the same day giving his approval, *"I have, undoubtedly, French Bill. He will be hanged at two o'clock in the afternoon tomorrow."*

Loge was captured on November 30, 1864, about sixteen miles from Harper's Ferry, dressed in gray uniform, and was tried on December 1 thru December 2nd upon the charges of desertion and joining the guerrilla band of White and Mosby, which the Union authorities stated infested Loudoun County and vicinity. He was found guilty by a drum-head Court Martial of both charges and sentenced to be hanged. The finding of the Court was approved, and the sentence was carried into execution at three o'clock in the afternoon, just outside the fortifications on December 2, 1864.

Loge was a fine looking young French Canadian man about twenty years old and had deserted from the Sixtieth and Fifty-third New York Infantry. The gallows was one of the old fashioned kind with a trap-door. Three thousand soldiers witnessed the sight as the Post band played. Upon reaching the scaffold, Loge made a short address in which he acknowledged that he was guilty of desertion but denied that he had ever been a robber. He further stated that he would pursue the same course under the same circumstances if he could escape, but *"although life was sweet to all,"* he was not afraid to die; that he was twenty years of age, and his face was the same then as fifteen years since. He died *"a Southern soldier, a brave man, and a Christian."*

His hands and feet were then bound and the rope was adjusted about his neck, a cap placed over his head, and he waved and kissed a small crucifix. Another witness stated it was the saddest scene he ever beheld and said French Bill also stated, *"He would like to see his Mother."*

A gauntlet however was dropped to the ground as a signal, and the Assistant Provost Marshal immediately severed the rope sustaining the trap, releasing Loge who fell about six feet, unfortunately landing on the balls of his feet causing him to strangle as he desperately tried to stand. French Bill begged them unmercifully, *"For God's sake to shoot him at once,"* to put him out of his misery. The hanging sentence was finally carried out when four men drug him back on the scaffold, had the trap door readjusted, re-knotted the rope; and he was again swung off. Death shortly ensued from strangulation. The bearing of Loge throughout was bold and defiant to the last.

In the end, on December 2, 1864, between two and three o'clock in the afternoon, Emile Loge, one of John Mobberly's fiercest guerillas, the infamous assassin French Bill, a known Union deserter was officially hanged at Bolivar Heights by Captain A. D. Pratt, Provost-Marshal of the Harper's Ferry District. General Stevenson sent a short message back to General Sheridan saying, *"French Bill has been hanged in accordance with orders."*

Colonel John S. Mosby disputed the claim that Loge was one of his men after the war stating that French Bill never rode with his Rangers.

63) Mosby's men kill Sergeant Flemon Anderson on December 24, 1864 at his mother's house – 41173 Bald Hill Road, Waterford (Private Property)

Flemon Anderson house (N39°13'23" W77°34'35")

On Christmas Eve 1864, Mrs. Charles Anderson held a special holiday social party at her residence, Edge Hill. The house had been initially built about 1770 and added onto in 1810. She was the widow of the late Union Captain Charles Anderson of the Loudoun Rangers, who had fallen to his death from a cliff in Bolivar Heights on November 1, 1863. Her son, Sergeant Flemon Anderson and two other sergeants in the Loudoun Rangers, John and George Hickman, were present with some other younger folks enjoying themselves. Anderson and the Hickmans had earlier that day been on a scout with Captain James Grubb on a reconnaissance. Sergeant Anderson was sitting beside a young lady who rumor had it, would one day be the future Mrs. Anderson.

Loudoun Ranger Sergeant Flemon Anderson. Courtesy John Souders and Anderson descendent Patti Neis

133

About nine o'clock that night, the house was surrounded by sixteen of Captain Elijah White's and Mosby's men. Ten of them entered the front door with drawn revolvers. Sergeant Anderson quickly leapt to escape by the side door to the dining room with it being nearby. As he arose, his saber hook caught in the chair back. In attempting to make his exit, the chair caught on the door casing. While trying to

Union Sergeants John and George Hickman

unhook himself, about ten shots were fired at him with three taking effect. With revolver in hand, he fired as he ran. As he gained the outside of the door, thinking he had finally made it to safety, he was shot through the head by several Confederate cavalrymen who had surrounded the dwelling. In falling, his mother caught him in her arms and he died in a few minutes. Poor Mrs. Anderson had now lost both her loving husband and her dear sweet son in that God forsaken war.

Sergeant Anderson had a quiet disposition, was well poised, and brave to recklessness. He was one of the best all-around soldiers in the entire command. John and George Hickman were made prisoners, taken to Richmond and confined in Libby prison, until they were exchanged in March 1865.

After they had surrendered, one of the Confederates wanted to shoot John Hickman for some alleged grievance; the Confederate snapped his revolver, but it miss-fired. George Hickman appealed to their chivalrous spirit, saying, *"We have surrendered like men and ask magnanimous treatment."* One of the Bradens of Mosby's command, who was related to the Andersons, interfered and put a stop to any further killings. Due to this appeal, both of the Hickmans would live to fight another day.

Mosby Ranger J. West Aldridge

Entrance to the dining room where Flemon Anderson got caught in a chair and was initially shot

The side door Anderson used to make his escape from the dining room

Anderson exited and died in his mother's arms outside of the house behind this Silver Maple tree

In this affair, the Confederates had three wounded—including Robert Chew, who would survive his wound and would continue to fight for Mosby. Eben Simpson, possibly a member of Lige White's Thirty-fifth Battalion Virginia Cavalry, the Comanches, was badly wounded. Other of Mosby's Rangers who were identified as fighting at the Anderson place were West Aldridge, Gabe Braden, and John Chew, the brother of Robert Chew.

Mosby Ranger Robert Chew

Captain James Grubb, of the Loudoun Rangers, left Waterford on his return at ten o'clock, arriving at Colonel William Giddings' at twelve o'clock midnight where he remained for the night and left at daylight the next morning, December 25th. Before arriving at Taylorstown, they learned of the sad and unfortunate affair at Mrs. Anderson's. While stopping to view for the last time the remains of Sergeant Anderson, who had marched by his side only a few hours before, the tears rolled down Captain Grubb's cheek.

Sergeant Anderson was buried in Union Cemetery at Waterford the next day, Monday, December 26, 1864. There would be no more Andersons riding with the Loudoun Rangers.

64) Last combat in Loudoun County on March 21, 1865 at Hamilton, Harmony, or Katy's Hollow – 150 yards South from Battle Peak Court on Sands Road, Hamilton

Katy's Hollow (N39°7'28" W77°40'19")

On Tuesday, at dawn on March 21, 1865, Mosby's command met at the little town of Hamilton, or as it was frequently called Harmony, a Quaker Settlement. The Quakers were successful farmers and were of course noncombatants and especially loyal to the United States government. One hundred and twenty-eight Rangers were present and moved off to the Quaker Church.

Mosby knowing of their loyalty did not hesitate to appropriate forage and crops from these people. Mosby also knew that these same gentle folk kept in close contact with the Union forces across the Potomac, so he did not trust them. He would be right about this. Mosby kept lookouts and pickets all around Hamilton.

Union Colonel Marcus A. Reno

137

After Mosby's men departed Harmony, the Union forces composed of cavalry and infantry commanded by Colonel Marcus Reno quickly occupied the town. A portion of Reno's cavalry came in sight of the church, but soon retired. Mosby moved off and halted about one mile south of Hamilton on the road to Lincoln. Captain Alfred Glascock, with Company D and a portion of Company A, was posted in a piece of woods to the left of the road. Five scouts, and later two better mounted Mosby men, were then ordered to ride forward and attack the Union advance and then fall back past the woods in which Glascock's men were concealed in order to draw out the Union cavalry from the infantry. The first five of Mosby's Rangers were identified as Bob Eastham, Jim Burgess, Townsend Vandevanter, Will Vandevanter, and John Adams. They were joined by Jacob Manning and Jim Wiltshire, the latter of whom took charge of them and brought on the collision.

Mosby Ranger Bob Eastham

Mosby Ranger Townsend Vandevanter

The scouts were very near the outskirts of the village when they encountered the Union force that had just turned out onto the Lincoln road. The ruse succeeded and the whole Union cavalry force started in pursuit of the now seven scouts, who fled wildly as though surprised and terror-stricken. John Adams horse ran against a tree and threw him. Before he could get up, the Yankees were upon him. John Chew and Wirt Binford were shot a half mile closer in to the village. And young James Keith was shot in the head and killed by the infantry's fire on the outskirts of the town.

On came Reno's cavalry, shouting and yelling, and their advance swept by before they noticed the Rangers. As they approached, Mosby ordered his hidden Rangers to fall back a little from the road so as to keep out of sight as much as possible as Wiltshire's party came dashing past. Some of the Rangers in the rear, not understanding this movement, created some confusion in the ranks. Noticing this, Captain Glascock said: *"Come, Company D! Come on Company A!"* and dashed on, followed by his men. They hurled themselves upon the flank and front of the astonished foe.

The roadway at once became congested. The Union cavalry stood for a short while, but only for a few minutes, then gave way and fled back towards Hamilton pursued by Glascock and his men who rained bullets among them. Not far from the woods, the road entered a narrow lane with a high steep bank on each side. Into this lane the panic-stricken men jammed themselves—men and horses pressed so tightly together that some time elapsed before they could get forward.

Colonel Mosby sat upon his horse in the field on top of the bank, his eyes flashing, his long black plume tossing in the wind, waving on his men, who with loud cheers followed up the chase. When the retreating Union cavalrymen reached a piece of woods close to Hamilton, they attempted a rally, and for a few seconds there was a hand to hand fight between the Rangers and the Union cavalry. Here was where the Rangers suffered a few men killed and wounded in combat.

Mosby Ranger
Lieutenant Channing M. Smith

When the Union cavalry were crowded in the lane, a new Mosby Ranger arrival, Lieutenant Channing M. Smith, was near Mosby on the bank and fired six shots into their ranks. Then, following Mosby, he galloped along their flank up to the woods and was soon exchanging shots at close range. Spurring his horse out into the road, he was attacked by two of the enemy, one of whom he killed when the other quickly wheeled and ran off. The fire of the infantry then became so hot that Colonel Mosby ordered the men to fall back.

Twenty-five Rangers not hearing or heeding the order went through both the Union cavalry and infantry. They were quickly repulsed by the deadly fire raining down on them from the concealed Union infantrymen and returned to the rest of the Rangers. Ranger James Sinclair insisted that he rode through the town, collected "tributes" from a Yankee soldier in the middle of the street, and rode out.

Mosby Ranger James Sinclair

Not more than sixty of the Rangers took part in the fight owing to the narrowness of the road, but the fight was sharp and desperate so far as the Rangers were concerned. The Union cavalry also acquitted themselves honorably in this affair, although surprised and forced to retreat.

Lieutenant Channing Smith acted independently in this fight and had good opportunity to see and judge the fighting qualities of Mosby's men for the first time. He came to the conclusion that the conscientious, brave soldier who loved the fierce excitement and danger of battle could be accommodated serving with Mosby. Smith also noticed Mosby's coolness, presence of mind, and courage in the heat of battle.

Mosby drew off his men and halted in a field in full view of the Union cavalry. The men cheered, waved their hats, and used every means to draw the cavalry away from the infantry. Some of Mosby's men who ventured too close to the enemy's lines were fired on, and one Ranger, Joseph Griffin, was wounded and his horse was killed. He attempted to gain the shelter of the woods, but was pursued and captured.

Fifteen of the Union cavalrymen were killed and a number were wounded, some mortally. Thirteen, including one lieutenant, were captured, together with fifteen horses. One Union Lieutenant Delose Chase was mortally wounded and was treated by a Quaker family in a brown stone house until he died. Mosby's loss was two killed, and James Keith and Wirt M. Binford. John A. Chew, Benton Fletcher, Jacob Manning, Benton Shipley and two or three others were wounded.

Lieutenant John H. Black, who commanded the Twelfth Pennsylvania Cavalry's vanguard, was also severely wounded in the battle. He was knocked from his saddle by a pistol ball that entered and lodged in the small of his back, paralyzing him from the waist down. The Rangers then stripped him of all his clothes and possessions except his pantaloons, shirt and drawers and left him for dead. Fortunately two local families cared for him, one after the other, until he was well enough to travel home. See Appendix B, Union Lieutenant John H. Black.

Union Lieutenant John H. Black

The battalion being ordered to meet next morning about three miles from Hamilton, moved off towards North Fork. The men scattered about in small squads and remained at farm houses in the neighborhood. Pickets were placed near and around the town to watch the movements of the enemy, who went into camp. The next day the Rangers went back to Hamilton, but the Union soldiers had gone to Snickersville. That would be the final chapter in the fighting at Hamilton.

In that encounter, Mosby had met Colonel Marcus Reno, with the Twelfth Pennsylvania Cavalry, which also just happened to be the last fight in which Mosby would be personally in command.

Reno would be rewarded for his engagement against Mosby with a commission to brigadier general, and afterward, enjoyed some notoriety in connection with the Custer massacre. Lastly, Reno would not forget his meeting with the Gray Ghost and the lessons he learned at Hamilton that may have saved his life at the Little Big Horn.

65) Possible house where Union Lieutenant John H. Black was treated March 21, 1865 – 17889 Sands Road, Hamilton (Private Property)

Possibly the house where Union Lieutenant John H. Black may have been treated (N39°7'19″ W77°40'43″)

66) Last combat in Loudoun County on March 21, 1865, Harmony Church – 380 East Colonial Highway, Hamilton

Harmony Church. It is believed Mosby's men stopped here when they first arrived in Hamilton (N39°7′59″ W77°39′18″)

67) Manassas Gap Railroad Marker – 17899 Sands Road, Hamilton

Manassas Gap Railroad Marker (N39°7′18″ W77°41′2″)

Marker in Katy's Hollow for the Loudoun Branch of the Manassas Gap Railroad that was never completed due to the war.

68) Downey's Mill and Stillhouse in March 1865 – Downey Mill Road, .1 mile west from Taylorstown Road, Taylorstown

Remains of Downey's Mill along Catoctin Creek (N39°15'14" W77°34'41")

The owner of Downey's Stillhouse, James M. Downey, was President of the bogus Virginia Senate, under the Pierpont dynasty, then holding its sessions in Alexandria. The place was a great rendezvous point for the Loudoun Rangers, at which they captured quite a number of Mosby's men also visiting the still; and from this place the Loudoun Rangers would come up to Waterford, a distance of only five miles away, to see their parents and sweethearts.

Near the end of March 1865, a detachment of Mosby's men were sent to Downey's Mill and had the still destroyed and poured the liquor into the creek. Mrs. Downey however determined to have her revenge. And she would get her revenge in a very short period of time.

Four Loudoun Rangers; Sergeant James H. Beatty, Henry Hough, Joe Ritchie, and George Davis, obtained permission to go to Loudoun on a scout. The river was high and the roads were muddy, so the boys left their horses at camp and went on foot. Near Downey's stillhouse, they struck the trail of three of Mosby guerillas; Mosby's Quartermaster J. James Wright, Major Hibbs, and John Bolling who went to Downey's a few

Loudoun Ranger George Davis

143

days after the destruction of the still to collect a tithe of bacon for themselves.

When Mosby's Rangers arrived at the still, they dismounted and went into the house and filled their canteens with whiskey. Sergeant Beatty and the other Loudoun Rangers took positions in the wagon shed. When the Confederates came out to get their horses, Sergeant Beatty's crew rushed out of the shed and opened fire on the enemy, capturing all three before they had time to draw their revolvers. The Loudoun Rangers accumulated eight revolvers and four excellent horses from their Confederate foe.

Mosby Ranger John Bolling

The Loudoun Rangers mounted their horses and marched the three Rangers ten paces in front, and in that order, they were taken across the Potomac River to Berlin, Maryland. It must have really been a sad day for poor old Hibbs. Not only was the still destroyed before he got there....He was captured to boot!

A few weeks later Sergeant Beatty, Henry Hough, and John Hickman of the Loudoun Rangers went back to Downey's. On entering the parlor, one of Mosby's men was sitting talking to Mrs. Downey. The Loudoun Rangers took charge of him and asked him where his arms were? The single Mosby Ranger pointed to a chair in a corner of the room and said, *"There they are."* He never tried to get them nor did he even care to do anything else.

Civil War era bottles

69) Formation of Company H, Forty-third Battalion Virginia Cavalry on April 5, 1865 at North Fork Church – 38104 North Fork Road, North Fork

North Fork Church c1857 (N39°3′36″ W77°41′8″)

A meeting was called on the fifth of April 1865 at the North Fork Church at which a large number of men assembled for the last of Mosby's elections. Mosby had just heard that Richmond had fallen and was much concerned about the news. In conversation with Sergeant John W. Corbin and Ranger J. Marshall Crawford he said, *"There is nothing else for me to do but to fight on."* The men declared they would stand by him.

A new Company was organized, and George Baylor, formerly of the Stonewall Brigade and later with the Twelfth Virginia Cavalry, was elected as captain. Edward "Ned" F. Thomson, from Fairfax County and identified by his family as the "executioner," was first lieutenant; James G. Wiltshire, from

Mosby Ranger John W. Corbin

145

Mosby Ranger George Baylor

Jefferson County, second lieutenant; and Benjamin Franklin Carter from Loudoun County was named third lieutenant; all elected unanimously due their meritorious conduct in battle and their promotion was regarded by all as a fitting recognition of their worth.

Captain Baylor, a native of Jefferson County, was a gallant officer who had distinguished himself on

Mosby Ranger Lieutenant Edward "Ned" Thomson

many a battlefield. Although a mere youth, by his daring and heroic conduct he had won the confidence and esteem of Lee, Stuart, and Wade Hampton. As a successful scout, he had no superior in the army. Therefore on all important and hazardous expeditions. Stuart and Hampton called on him to execute which he did exceptionally. Baylor's fame was not confined to the Confederate army but extended to that of the enemy. The foe in the Valley dreaded Baylor as much as they did Mosby. Mosby had been for a long time anxious to have Baylor attached to his command. Company H was organized especially for Captain Baylor.

After the election, Colonel Mosby complimented the men on their choice of officers and told them they could now go and do something to distinguish themselves.

Baylor's first foray was the very next day at Key Switch in West Virginia where Company H, with fifty-two men, virtually annihilated the Union's Loudoun Rangers without a single Ranger killed. Baylor killed five or six Union

Mosby Ranger Benjamin Franklin Carter

Rangers, captured forty-five, over seventy horses together with their arms and equipment. Baylor only had one man wounded, Frank Helm, of Warrenton, sustaining his injury as he charged among the foremost into the camp.

When General Winfield S. Hancock, so distinguished in the Union Army, heard of Baylor's exploit, he laughed heartily and exclaimed, *"Well, that is the last of the Loudoun Rangers."*

North Fork Church

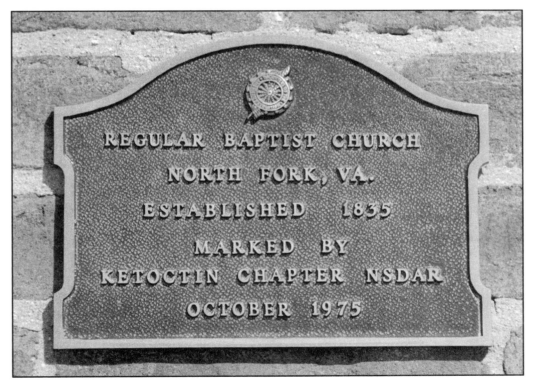

North Fork Church Marker

John S. Mosby Signature on letter given to North Fork Church Chaplain Parker C. Thompson

70) Isaac Burns Anderson joins Company H, Forty-third Battalion Virginia Cavalry on April 5, 1865. Lived at 19453 Ebenezer Church Road, Round Hill

Mosby Ranger Isaac "Ike" Anderson House (N39°4'38" W77°48'16")

Isaac "Ike" Burns Anderson enrolled as a private in Company B, Twelfth Virginia Cavalry on September 25, 1862, at Charles Town, (West) Virginia. According to his Confederate tombstone, Anderson was born June 21, 1841, although some historians have him enlisting at sixteen years old.

At one point during the war, Anderson, and a few other members of the Twelfth Virginia Cavalry, was detailed to guard captured sheep. He was wounded in action near Fisher's Hill at Tom's Brook, Virginia on October 9, 1864 when he was shot through the lungs and was carried from the field. Captain George Baylor referred to Private Anderson as a gallant member of the company. Anderson was involved in the raid on Charles Town, West Virginia on April 14, 1865, towards the end of the war.

Mosby Ranger Isaac "Ike" Anderson

Anderson joined Mosby's command around late March 1865 along with Captain George Baylor of the Twelfth Virginia Cavalry. Anderson participated in the Mosby scout to the Shenandoah Valley, and the train derailment of the Baltimore and Ohio train near Charles Town, West Virginia in March 1865. Anderson was also involved in the Mosby attack on the block-house at Summit Point, Jefferson County, West Virginia on March 30, 1865. Before the war, Ike lived in Maryland for an unknown period of time.

After the war, Ike lived as a farmer near Round Hill in Loudoun County. Anderson's parents were Harrison A. Anderson and Mary Ann Burns of Jefferson County, (West) Virginia. Ike married his wife Virginia (Jennie) A. Furr right after the war on November 15, 1866. They had ten children, six girls and four boys.

After the war Anderson, was approved for a Confederate pension of fifty dollars. Anderson would also attend various Confederate and Mosby reunions from 1910 to the 1920s and was very proud of his service in the Confederate army. He died in Arlington, Virginia, June 22, 1923 and was buried in Ebenezer Church, in Loudoun County.

It should also be noted that he was a cousin of the famous Confederate female spy, Belle Boyd, who is known to have aided the efforts of the Confederate Second Corps commander Lieutenant General Thomas Jonathan "Stonewall" Jackson.

Elderly Isaac "Ike" Anderson

Colonel John S. Mosby

**71) The killing of Confederate John Mobberly, April 5, 1865, Civil War Trail Marker –
36888 Breaux Vineyards Lane, Purcellville**

John W. Mobberly Civil War Trail Marker (N39°13'53" W77°43'59")

On April 1, 1865, Brigadier General John D. Stevenson, the Union Commander at Harper's Ferry, wrote to the chief of staff General Winfield S. Hancock, determined to get rid of the notorious murderer and killer John W. Mobberly.

> *"There is a gang of murderers infesting Loudoun, who have done incalculable service for the rebels for the last four years. The leader of the band is named Mobberly, and is one of Mosby's right hand men (which was not true, editor's comment). Some citizens of Loudoun have proposed to me that if I will arm them and give them the means of living away from home for a while they will kill or capture the band.*
>
> *The band consists of Mobberly, Jim Riley, S. Mocks and Tribbey. All of them have murdered our soldiers time and again. The band originally consisted of about fifteen men. During the last summer we have killed most of the band, leaving these four men, who are the head devils of the concern.*
>
> *I think promising these men a reward of $1,000 for Mobberly and $500 for each of the others, dead or alive, will clean out the concern. The Government could readily afford to pay $50,000 for them and save the amount in the prevention of the destruction of public property in six months' operations of the band."*

General Hancock approved the venture, but objected to offering a reward openly. He stated that the parties would be rewarded in proportion of their services.

The Union authorities knew that they had to come up with an adequate bait to lure Mobberly into a trap. Funny as it may sound, a horse was selected; because it was well known that Mobberly was a good judge of horse flesh, and that Luther H. Potterfield, who lived at the foot of the Short Hills about four miles west of Lovettsville, had a fine fast horse for sale to any man who could meet his price.

Mobberly soon heard about that fine mare, and against his mother's wishes rode, over the mountain with his friend Jim Riley to take a closer look for himself at that fine steed. The Potterfield barn sat on a slight slope not far from the farm lane. A small stream crossed the lane that led to the main road about a quarter mile from the barn. Unbeknownst to Mobberly, three Union troopers learned from reliable sources that Mobberly was going to visit the Potterfield farm on April 5, 1865.

One of the Union men concealed in the Potterfield barn was Sergeant Charles B. Stewart, the man Mobberly had shot point blank in the face and left to die at Waterford in May 1864. But Stewart had survived this ordeal and had vowed his revenge.

Around noon, on April 5, 1865 as expected, Mobberly and Riley turned into the farm lane and rode toward the barn. When they reached the stream that crossed the lane, Mobberly anxious to see the horse, rode toward the barn with Riley stopping to water his mare.

Mobberly continued to ride and had to pass through the barnyard. In doing so, Mobberly rode up to the gate and reached over and raised the latch and saw someone standing in the window with his carbine drawn upon him.

What happened next has been debated by several historians with many different scenarios. The best story is that three Union troopers suddenly burst from the barn with pistols cocked demanding Mobberly's surrender. Mobberly realizing there was nowhere to escape exclaimed, *"Oh Lord, I'm gone."* And true to Mobberly's belief, three shots rang out, two penetrating his skull killing him instantly and toppling him from his horse.

The second version had Union soldiers firing from their concealed positions within the barn as soon as Mobberly rode within range, but heard the clicks as the guns were being cocked and exclaimed, *"Oh Lord, I'm gone,"* before the deadly death shots rang out. Since Mobberly had quite a reputation as a shootist, this version does have some credence with historians.

Nevertheless, it is generally believed that Sergeant Stewart is the man credited with killing Mobberly. Jim Riley, who had stopped to water his horse, witnessed the execution and rode at a full gallop towards his home in the Short Hills. While racing there, he passed Mobberly's mother and told her they had been ambushed at the Potterfield farm and that her son was badly wounded.

Mrs. Mobberly started at once to the farm to find out the condition of her son. When she arrived at the farm, she found a large pool of blood in the barnyard, but there was no body. There were droplets of blood sporadically located on the road towards Harper's Ferry, because the body had been thrown across the horse's back, "like a sack of grain and conveyed to Harper's Ferry."

Mobberly's body had been taken to army headquarters and was displayed in the front of the building on Shenandoah Street in Harper's Ferry. Word quickly spread that the notorious murderer was at last no longer breathing. As the soldiers rushed to view the body, many Union men grotesquely started to denude Mobberly's body by hacking off strips of his clothing for mementoes. It was even reported that some Union men dug out small pieces of human flesh as relics and keepsakes.

General Stevenson gleefully sent a telegram to the Honorable Edwin M. Stanton, Secretary of War and said:

> *"I have sent out on Monday, a small party to wipe out the notorious guerilla, Mobberly and his band. They returned today with the body of Mobberly, and in the fight mortally wounded his right-hand man, Riley"* (which was not true, editor's comment).

The very next day, Mobberly's friends obtained some measure of revenge when they visited the Potterfield farm and burned the barn and everything in it. The Government reimbursed the Potterfield's for the loss of the barn with $2,500. The men that assisted and provided information for the trap received $1,000, but unfortunately the Union men who did the actual killing received nothing but a hearty thank you from the Union army.

The legend of John W. Mobberly still lives in Loudoun County today.

72) Mosby crossing point into Maryland at Conrad's Ferry – White's Ferry Road, Leesburg

Today's White's Ferry was known as Conrad's Ferry throughout that four year conflict. The ferry had been a major crossing point for Union and Confederate units traversing from Loudoun County, Virginia to Montgomery County, Maryland. As early as 1861, the ferry was occupied by the First New Hampshire Infantry, a three month regiment which constructed the first earthworks to defend the ferry. Also, Colonel Edward Baker's Brigade would occupy the Poolesville area and Conrad's Ferry earlier in the war.

Conrad's Ferry remained occupied periodically by Union troops throughout the war. Mosby's Rangers would cross at Conrad's Ferry whenever the Union troops would depart. Generally too deep for fording by infantry or artillery, it was a perfect crossing location for Union and Confederate cavalry, especially Mosby's Rangers. It was definitely a favorite crossing used by Lieutenant Colonel Elijah "Lige" White and his Thirty-fifth Battalion Virginia Cavalry, known as the Comanches. The Comanches conducted various raids into the Poolesville area, which was the birthplace of Elijah White. White would cross into Maryland by White's Ford and return from these raids by using the one that was not guarded. John Singleton Mosby and his Rangers used Conrad's as well, crossing into Maryland there while Jubal Early marched towards Washington City in July 1864. A few days later, General McCausland's cavalry crossed back into Virginia at Conrad's attempting to cut-off Early who was using a different route.

White's Ferry from the Virginia Side (N39°9'19" W77°31'23")

Just south of White's or Conrad's Ferry was Conrad's Ford, which later was changed to White's Ford after Elijah White, on whose Loudoun farm is where the ford is located. Colonel White was well known to everyone in Montgomery County, Maryland, and Loudoun County, Virginia. Unfortunately for the Union forces camped in the area, they had never heard of Lige White early in the war. White's Ford was the site of three major Confederate crossings of the Potomac from Virginia into Montgomery County during the war. From September 4, 5, and 6, 1862 over thirty-five thousand Confederates belonging to the First and Second Corps of the Army of Northern Virginia, commanded by Generals James Longstreet and Stonewall Jackson under Robert E. Lee, crossed into Maryland at White's Ford on its way to the bloodiest day in American history at Sharpsburg on September 17, 1862.

J.E.B. Stuart's cavalry re-crossed into Virginia at the end of his second ride around McClellan's army in October 1862 embarrassing the whole Union Army; and General Early entered White's Ford in his retreat from Washington City in July 1864.

154

Mosby's Rangers would traverse White's Ford on a routine basis during the entire two and a half years that they rode as a guerilla unit. On one raid during the period October 14-16, 1864, William Chapman with eighty Rangers crossed at White's Ford, capturing and destroying about ten or twelve canal boats loaded with cargo and then moved to Adamstown, Maryland where they encountered, ambushed, and routed the Union Loudoun Rangers before going back to Virginia.

73) Mortimer Lane captured by Union troops, date unknown – 43280 John Mosby Highway, Chantilly

Lane House c1965 (N38°55'28" W77°30'20")

Mortimer Lane, of Mosby's Command, was captured by Union cavalry around this isolated house on the Little River Turnpike at an unknown date while searching for food and forage. Lane was taken to the prison camp at Point Lookout, Maryland and survived the war. Lane died in late June or early July 1910, aged sixty-seven years old, and is buried in an unmarked grave at Frying Pan Church.

Another incident occurred at this location when a group of Mosby's men went to the home of a black man living nearby who had been observed talking with Union cavalry on several occasions. There they proceeded to hang him from a tree in his front yard, making his family observe his death. The tree used for the hanging, which was located along Route 50, was destroyed by the Department of Virginia Transportation around 2005.

Lane House (N38°55'28" W77°30'20")

74) Snickersville Turnpike Marker – 41079 Snickersville Turnpike, Aldie

Snickersville Turnpike Marker (N38°58′53″ W77°39′5″)

This historic marker is located along the Snickersville Turnpike. Mosby and his Rangers traveled this road many times during the Civil War.

75) Bluemont Historic Village Marker – 33716 Snickers Gap Road, Intersection of Clayton Mill Road and Snickers Gap Road, Bluemont

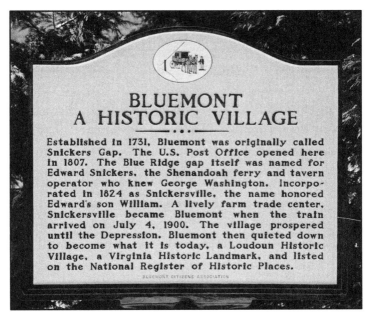

Bluemont Historic Village Marker (N39°6'40″ W77°50'4″)

This historic Marker is located in Bluemont. This location was visited by Mosby and his Rangers throughout the Civil War.

76) *Old Welbourne* – 21398 Willisville Road, Bluemont (Private Property)

Old Welbourne (N39°1'48″ W77°49'40″)

John Peyton Dulany, who was born at *Clermont*, in Fairfax County, Virginia married Mary Ann deButts in 1810 at *Mount Welby* in Maryland. Dulany's mother gave him a tract of land, five hundred and three acres of sweet fertile soil in Loudoun County, on which he built a small log cabin. He called it *Welbourne* in honor of his bride's ancestral home in England. It was a simple home, "only two little rooms below and the same above," and far different from John Peyton's childhood home or the fine Maryland estate of *Mount Welby* where Mary Ann had grown up. In 1833, the Dulany's bought a far more grand home from Mrs. Joanna Lewis, which lay not far away…right across the road from Mary Ann's brother Richard deButts, at *Crednal*. Again, the twosome named their new home *Welbourne Hall*, so their log cabin and its lands soon became known as *Old Welbourne*.

Old Welbourne stayed in the Dulany family for over one hundred and fifty years before it was sold to a non-relative. Only a chimney and crumbling roof beams covered with vines remain of John Peyton Dulany's log cabin today. It is hidden away behind a cornfield and sheltered by old trees. Generations of his descendants; Dulanys, deButtses, Roszels, Halls, Whitings, and Tayloes rest in a cemetery shaded by old hemlock trees and surrounded by a sturdy rock wall.

John deButts, who rode with the Gray Ghost and the Forty-third Battalion Virginia Cavalry, was also laid to rest in that burial ground.

77) Mosby's men play cards in Hillsboro – Route 9 and Hillsboro Road, Hillsboro

Hillsboro, Virginia (N39°11'53″ W77°43'14″)

Around the end of May to June 1, 1864, Mosby had received word that the enemy had laid a trap in Loudoun to capture him; and he, being a person ever ready to find out what the Union army was doing, ordered a meeting of the command at Upperville. One hundred of Mosby's men reported to duty. Captain Adolphus "Dolly" Richards, with Company B, was sent ahead to the neighborhood of Point of Rocks, to try and summon the enemy over the river, while Mosby took Companies A and C with him to establish an ambush. The Ranger's movements were made under cover of night, the main roads being shunned to avoid being seen, and to keep the people ignorant of the Ranger's actual strength.

Captain Adolphus "Dolly" Richards

In the daytime, the Rangers stayed in the woods and were not allowed to expose themselves to anyone. Reaching the turnpike leading to Berlin, Mosby distributed his men in squads along this thoroughfare, in striking distance of each other, and patiently awaited the approach of the enemy to strike. Captain Richards, being unable to draw the enemy across the river from their stronghold at Point of Rocks, Mosby and ten men went to Harper's Ferry to attempt to draw them out from that place. The men had not smelt gunpowder for nearly one month now and were "spoiling for a fight."

Company B was ordered to Hillsboro in hopes that the enemy could be aroused from the Ferry to fight. In such a contingency, they were to hold the attacking Union force in check until the rest of the Rangers could be brought up. Company B remained at Hillsboro for three long days with no signs of an attack. Mosby returned to Fauquier, and to this day the Rangers never learned the Union plan for trapping Mosby and his men.

During Company's B stay in Hillsboro, they were most hospitably entertained by some of their citizens. Mr. Janney's and Mr. Hoe's accomplished wives and daughters were unremitting in their attentions to Richards and his men; and music, dancing, card-playing and any other type of amusement was the order for three whole days.

However, drinking was never mentioned by anyone during that three day holiday. But you can bet that Richards had a hard time keeping some of his men away from the bottle.

78) Lovettsville Civil War Marker – 12930 Lutheran Church Road, Lovettsville

Lovettsville Civil War Marker (N39°15'31" W77°38'22")

Lovettsville, like Waterford, was very sympathetic to the Union cause and had many men who served in the Loudoun Rangers.

79) *Stoke* – Champe Ford Hill and Route 50, Middleburg

Stoke (N38°58'4" W77°39'54")

Stoke is a beautiful mansion house that was built on a hillside overlooking the Aldie countryside in 1791 off of Champe Ford Road.

Around 1821, *Stoke* was owned by Colonel Lewis Berkeley and his wife Frances Noland. Colonel Berkeley had five children, Molly, William, Edmund, Norborne, and Charles Fenton. By 1861, Norborne Berkeley would be the owner of *Stoke*. All four sons would become officers in the Eighth Virginia Infantry and serve honorably for the entire four year period. Edmund Berkeley would obtain the rank of lieutenant colonel; William N. would make major; Norborne would become colonel; and Charles Fenton would become captain. No other Confederate unit of any kind would be so dominated in the officer ranks as the Berkeley family was in the Bloody Eighth!

Also, the hillside where *Stoke* is situated is called by longtime residents in the area as Mosby's Hill, because it was thought to be a great observation post for the Gray Ghost and his Rangers. Mosby could watch the Union wagon and troop movements going back and forth all along the Little River Turnpike.

The people living in *Stoke* claim that Mosby was either wounded or was shot at in the house during that bloody four year war. The story goes… one day a Union soldier burst through the front door, flew up the staircase, suddenly wheeled around on the top landing to shoot a rebel he thought was Colonel John S. Mosby. But the bullet missed its mark and hit the casing of the drawing room door where its imprint remains to this day. No time period is given, and there are no other names mentioned except for the good Colonel's.

The authors have been unable to find any other additional documentation concerning this incident. However, there is documentation that Mrs. Robert E. Lee visited the mansion and was able to walk into the place unassisted, but soon after she would be crippled with arthritis.

80) Mosby's Hill (Observation Point for Mosby throughout the war overlooking Little River Turnpike) – Champe Ford Hill and Route 50, Middleburg

Mosby has been said to frequently ride up on this hill overlooking the Little River Turnpike in Middleburg to listen and look for Union wagons and troops passing along the road during the war.

Mosby's Hill (N38°58′4″ W77°39′54″)

161

81) *Mosby Spring Farm*, house of James Wiltshire – 36042 Route 50, Middleburg (Private Property)

Mosby Spring Farm, house of James Wiltshire (N38°58′4″ W77°45′34″)

Deserted and surrounded by old trees and brush, which offered cover and forage, and a flowing spring that provided fresh water for their horses, this cottage was an ideal hiding place for Mosby's Rangers staying in Mosby's Confederacy. Lieutenant James Girard Wiltshire would visit this cottage on many occasions during and after the war. It is very possible that this cottage was the safe house where Jim and his brother Charley Wiltshire stayed while serving with John Singleton Mosby. Unfortunately, poor Charley would be mortally wounded in action at the Daniel Bonham place outside of Berryville on March 30, 1865. He would linger about four days before he finally passed away. Jim Wiltshire would survive the war and would become a very respected and active member of the community.

Ranger Wiltshire was just twenty-one years old when the war ended, but he was commissioned an officer in Company H, and was a gallant and brave man throughout the war. Wiltshire is recognized with firing and wounding the last Union cavalryman by a Mosby Ranger in the fight at Arundel's Tavern on April 10, 1865.

After firing one of the final shots in anger, Wiltshire dreamed to become a medical doctor but was not sure if that was possible. Money was a serious issue in the eighteen sixties, especially in Virginia and Maryland after four long years of violent hostilities. He had no money. But

Wiltshire still had an ace up his sleeve. He had been involved in the Greenback Raid where Mosby had divided up approximately $173,000 in which each Ranger on the raid got $2,200 from the loot taken from a Union passenger train in October 1864. Wiltshire did not waste nor spend his loot he was given. He took it back to this family summer home in Manpike, West Virginia, telling only a trusted black servant of its whereabouts while hiding it in the trunk of an old tree for safe keeping.

Returning at war's end, he prayed that his Union greenbacks would still be there and they were. Thus, the spoils of war enabled a young Confederate officer to achieve his lifelong dream to go to medical school and become a certified doctor. The money from the Greenback Raid not only paid his way through a very difficult two-year course of study at the Maryland Medical College (now John Hopkins), but assisted him immeasurably in setting up his own practice after graduation in Baltimore, Maryland.

Dr. James Wiltshire went on to become a renowned physician and marry the beautiful Frances Hill of Culpeper, who was related to Confederate General Ambrose Powell Hill.

It is also rumored, that the spirit of a teenage rebel has been roaming through the stone walls of the *Mosby Spring Farm* cottage periodically since the end of that war. Currently, the cottage is owned by George Wiltshire a descendant of the Wiltshire's who rode with the Gray Ghost.

82) *Welbourne* – 22314 Welbourne Farm Lane, Middleburg (Private Property)

Welbourne (N39°0'9" W77°48'46")

Welbourne is an old homestead enlarged over a century and a half to meet the tastes and needs of five generations of the same family. John Peyton Dulany purchased the nucleus of the present house, an eighteenth century stone farm dwelling in 1819, and enlarged it into a five-bay Federal style structure. The house was further enlarged many different times over the next hundred years.

Colonel Richard Henry Dulany lived in the house before and after the War Between the States. Richard Dulany rode off on a June morning in 1861 leaving behind his seventy-three year old father, John Peyton Dulany, in charge of a vast plantation, in addition to his five children ranging in age from four to eleven, assorted relatives, a tutor, nursemaid, servants, and over fifty slave families. Dulany would obtain the rank of colonel and would raise and outfit with uniforms and rifles his own cadre of soldiers, known as the Dulany Troop. Later he would later command the famous Laurel Brigade. Dulany would be wounded in battle three times and would survive the war.

 Brigadier General William H. Payne, formerly of the famous Black Horse Troop out of Warrenton, wrote about Colonel Dulany and his service after the war:

> *"I do not exaggerate when I say that there is no man in the State of Virginia whose splendid generosity, loyal patriotism and gallantry as a soldier I have more respect for, than I have for you. You plunged instantly into the melee…staking fortune, home and everything upon the result …and you fought to the finish.*
>
> *I was always struck not only with your gallantry, but with the fact that wound after wound was never used by you as a means of retiring from the conflict, but as soon as you could crawl from a sick bed you were in the saddle again. To me, you have become….an ideal man."*

During the four year ordeal Mosby and his Rangers found food and shelter there on many occasions, as did General J.E.B. Stuart and many other Confederate officers. A sad day for the family was when John Peyton Dulany died of diphtheria. His son was off fighting in the war.

Major John Pelham, known as "The Gallant Pelham," was the epitome of the Confederate cavalier. Twenty-three years old, he was handsome and a dandy with the ladies. He was the envy of many a man for the loving attention he gained from the young maidens in Virginia. One day, when Pelham was staying at *Welbourne,* he etched an inscription on the window that is still visible today. Also, young Private D. French Dulany used *Welbourne* as his safe house because he was related to the family. Unfortunately, Private Dulany would lose his life in a

Confederate John Pelham

164

gunfight with the Second Massachusetts Cavalry in Herndon in June 1864. Rangers John P. deButts, Boyd Smith and Thomas W. Turner also used *Welbourne* as a safe house. Major Heros von Borke, a Prussian who served on Stuart's staff, returned to America to visit his old comrades and stayed at Welbourne in June 1884. The history of this plantation house is everywhere to see!

83) The War Horse monument, The National Sporting Library & Museum – 301 The Plains Road, Middleburg

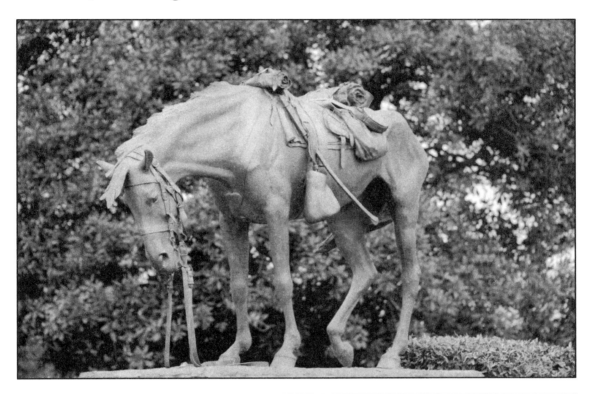

Monument to the Civil War Horse, The National Sporting Library & Museum (N38°58′0″ W77°44′19″)

This beautiful bronze sculpture created by Ted Pullan entitled "The War Horse" stands elegantly in front of the National Sporting Library in Middleburg, one of the most visited tourist attractions in that quaint little hamlet. Donated by the late philanthropist and horse lover Paul Mellon, the inscription reads, "In memory of the one and one-half million horses and mules of the Confederate and Union Armies who were killed, wounded, or died from disease in the Civil

165

War." The horse's head hangs low, somehow reflecting both the tragedy of that horrific conflict and the wear and tear on the various animals that suffered daily during those four years of constant usage.

84) Ranger George Dodd house – 22857 Carters Farm Lane, Middleburg (Private Property)

George Dodd house. The left side was built in 1790. The right side in 1910. (N38°59′37″ W77°41′26″)

Trap Door in family room of the George Dodd House

Mosby Ranger George Y. Dodd was a private in Company D when he enlisted in July 1864. During the war, he had a trap door built into his house in Middleburg leading to crawl space under the house should he or any of his comrades need to use it. He would eventually move to Fairfax County and file for a Confederate pension after the war.

85) Hibbs Bridge & Marker – 21005 Snickersville Gap Road at Hibbs Bridge Road and Snickersville Gap Road, Purcellville

Hibbs Bridge (N38°2′13″ W77°43′20″)

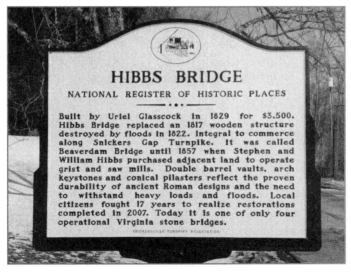

Hibbs Bridge Marker

Hibbs Bridge was built in 1829 by Uriel Glasscock replacing an 1817 wooded structure. William Hibbs, who was known as Major Hibbs, when he served with Colonel John S. Mosby, purchased adjacent land to operate a grist and saw mill.

86) Loudoun Rangers lived in Taylorstown – Taylorstown Road and Downey Mill Road
   Taylorstown

Village of Taylorstown Marker (N39°15'17" W77°34'36")

Taylorstown Historical Marker (N39°15'17" W77°34'36")

Taylorstown and Downey's Mill was visited throughout the war by the Confederate deserter John Mobberly, the Union's Loudoun Rangers, and Colonel John S. Mosby's Partisan Command for foraging excursions, military raids, and also daily visits to Downey's Stillhouse, an extremely popular stop for both sides fighting in the war.

87) *Rose Hill* **– 34064 Route 50, Upperville (Private Property)**

Rose Hill (N38°58′58″ W77°49′42″)

Rose Hill was built about 1820 by Amos Denham who purchased the land for $2,504. The house was used as an Inn and was located along the Ashby Gap road (now John Mosby Highway, Route 50) between Middleburg and Upperville and was a popular stage stop.

Union Colonel Strong Vincent and his Eighty-third Pennsylvania Infantry camped there in June 1863. *Rose Hill* was also visited by Major General J.E.B. Stuart and Colonel John S. Mosby, who it is rumored often found shelter and comfort within its walls. The barns were burned and its provisions and crops were often stolen by roving Union marauders and other scallywags.

Today's John Mosby Highway, or Route 50, was known as the Little River Turnpike during the war

88) Goose Creek Bridge and Marker – Route 50, west of Rector's Crossroads, Atoka

Goose Creek Bridge (N38°58′54″ W77°49′15″)

The Goose Creek Stone Bridge is the longest of the remaining early stone turnpike bridges in Northern Virginia. The exact construction date of the massive four-span structure has not been determined, but it may date as early as 1810. It is documented that tolls were collected on the Goose Creek Bridge as early as 1820.

Heavy fighting occurred on it and on both sides of the bridge during the cavalry fighting around Middleburg and Upperville between Confederate Major General J.E.B. Stuart and Union Major General Alfred Pleasanton on June 21, 1863. Large numbers of Union soldiers were killed and wounded while attempting to cross the Goose Creek Stone Bridge that day.

Goose Creek Stone Bridge was frequently crossed by Mosby's Rangers and Union cavalry attempting to capture or kill the Gray Ghost.

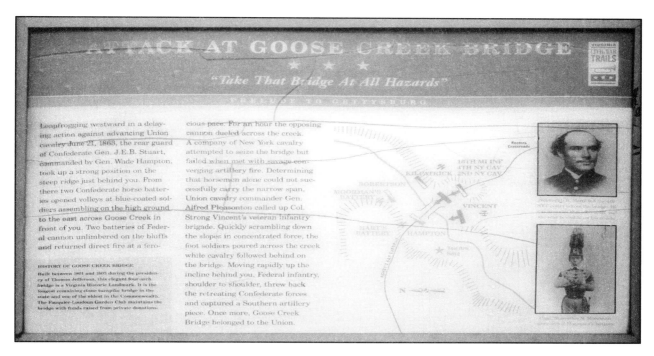

Goose Creek Bridge Marker

Trace of Little River Turnpike leading to Goose Creek Bridge – 34428 John Mosby Highway (N38°58′50″ W77°49′5″)

89) Dick Moran cemetery & marker, Brambleton Golf Course – 42180 Ryan Road, Ashburn

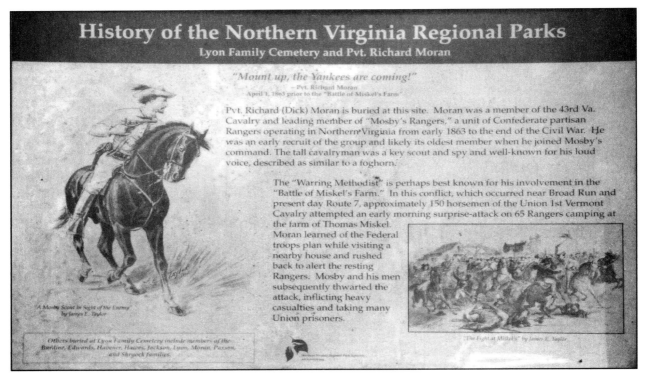

Dick Moran Marker, Brambleton Golf Course

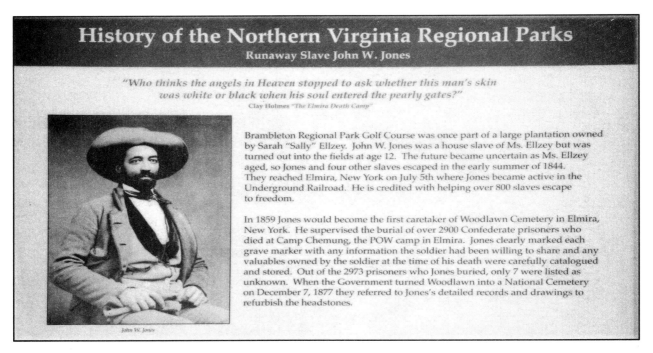

Brambleton Regional Park Marker, Brambleton Golf Course (N38°59'29" W77°32'26")

Dick Moran cemetery, Brambleton Golf Course

The area encompassing the Brambleton Golf Course in Ashburn, Loudoun County is also known as Wax Pool. Located inside the golf course is an old family cemetery where Mosby Ranger Richard Y. "Dick" Moran is buried in an unmarked grave. However, the golf course created a plaque documenting Dick Moran, also known by some of Mosby's Rangers as "Fog Horn" due to his extremely loud voice, verifying his burial at that site.

Dick Moran was possibly the oldest Ranger who ever served honorably in the Forty-third Battalion Virginia Cavalry. It is believed that he was between forty-nine to fifty-four years old, six feet one inches tall, shallow complexion, snow grey eyes, and grey hair. He had ten children when he joined the Rangers.

At the formation of Mosby's independent command before Mosby established company A, Moran was also one of the most feared men serving with that Partisan unit. He is famous for bellowing the frantic alarm at Miskell's Farm warning Mosby and his Rangers that, *"The Yankees are coming!"*

He was involved in some of the more harrowing and exciting escapades involving Colonel Mosby, and here are a few of those engagements where he played a major role and the dates where he was captured and imprisoned: the Fairfax Court House Raid on March 9, 1863; the Saint Patrick's Day Raid on March 17, 1863 in Herndon; the Miskell's Farm fight on April 1,

173

1863 (Harry Hatcher would save Moran's life in that encounter with a Union trooper); wounded and captured at Warrenton Junction on May 3, 1863; arrived at Old Capitol Prison on May 27, 1863; captured a second time in Loudoun County on June 17, 1863; transferred to Point Lookout on August 23, 1863; paroled at Point Lookout on April 27, 1864; captured by Blazer's Scouts at Myers Ford on September 4, 1864; and sent to Fort Warren, Massachusetts on February 6, 1865. Moran took the oath of allegiance to the United States on June 15, 1865 after the war at Fort Warren and returned to Wax Pool, Loudoun County to live out his final years.

Fog Horn Moran was an older gentleman, but he was a ferocious fighter in battle. If it had not been for Mosby forming a Partisan guerilla unit in Northern Virginia, no one would have ever known the fighting qualities and heroic actions of this notorious Ranger.

90) Bloomfield (near Ebenezer Church) – Airmont and Bloomfield Roads, Bloomfield

Bloomfield Marker (N39°3'15" W77°49'8")

Bloomfield was an important rendezvous point for Mosby's men because it was close to Snickersville, Round Hill, and Leesburg. Listed below are a few instances when the Rangers met at Bloomfield:

Major Thomas Gibson, Fourteenth Pennsylvania Cavalry reported that Mosby's entire command was last camped at Bloomfield between April 21 to24, 1864.

On October 16, 1864, Mosby's Command met at Bloomfield. Companies C, E, and F remained to operate along the railroad. Mosby with companies A, B, and D went on a raid into Fairfax County.

On October 24, 1864, Mosby's Command met at Bloomfield. Nearly 400 men reported for duty.

On November 17, 1864, the first squadrons of Companies A and B, under command of Captain Dolly Richards met at Bloomfield to begin their search for Blazer's Scouts. They would eliminate Blazer's Scouts the next day at Kabletown.

On January 30, 1865, Mosby met with thirty men at Bloomfield and went on a raid on the Baltimore and Ohio Railroad, between Harper's Ferry and Winchester.

91) *Llangollen***, safehouse and the home of Martin Maddux – 21515 Trappe Road, Upperville (Private Property)**

Llangollen (N39°1′27″ W77°52′37″)

Llangollen was the home of Ranger Martin Maddux and his son Henry Cabell "Cab" Maddux who joined Mosby's Rangers when he was only fourteen years old. *Llangollen* was a beautiful mansion that was also used as a safe house for boarding Mosby's Rangers and was located about four miles west of Upperville. Rangers Joseph Bryan, Frank Fox, Charlie H. Dear, Coley Jordan, James L. McIntosh, Edwin "Ned" Gibson, and John H. Thomas stayed there during the war.

Returning to *Llangollen* after a raid on October 26, 1864, Joe Bryan stated to Charlie Dear, *"Charlie Dear, I do firmly believe you have been trying to get me killed, and I have had no rest or very little sleep since I joined. It is 'Get up, Richards or Montjoy is waiting at the gate, and says come on.'"*

Bryan further stated, *"Haven't I been with you all the time by your side?"* Dear said, *"Yes, but this has been awful work today on my nerves."*

Ned Gibson jumped into the conversation, *"This is what you caught by going with this set. You will have to get used to it if you are to ride between Charlie Dear and myself at the head of Company D behind Montjoy."*

Also in the *Llangollen* household were Mrs. Evelina Hefflebower, the sister of Martin Maddux and her two little granddaughters; "bad Bet" and "pretty little Mollie." Mrs. Hefflebower would stuff Joseph Bryan's last shirt up the chimney to save it from some pillaging Yankees.

The shocks, fears, and constant strain upon the faith and strength of soul, mind, and body of the mothers and dependents of Mosby's Confederacy cannot be told nor imagined. In late November or early December 1864, Mrs. Maddux and Mrs. Hefflebower with their children, dragged all their movable belongings into the yard while they witnessed their neighbors' homes and mills in flames, and they were told by Sheridan's troopers that their home would be burned during the now infamous "burning raid."

Fortunately, *Llangollen* was never wrecked or destroyed. Such fiery night raids and fearful moments of a surprise visit by Union cavalry seeking to either rob, steal, or to harass and scare women and children caused a great deal of fear and anxiety to the civilian population in and around *Llangollen*.

On August 18, 1913, Colonel John S. Mosby visited *Llangollen* again for the last time when he was invited and entertained by the owner H.A. Toulmain. *Llangollen* was where the colonel so often stopped during the war and one can only imagine the memories of war Mosby must have been feeling when he walked around this stately mansion situated at the foot of the Blue Ridge Mountains.

Colonel John S. Mosby

92) Mosby Rangers buried in Ebenezer Church Cemetery – 20427 Airmont Road, Bluemont
(N39°8′27″ W77°48′41″)

Mosby Ranger Isaac Burns
Anderson

Mosby Ranger Francis Elias

Mosby Ranger Joshua Fletcher

Mosby Ranger Thomas Rector

**93) Mosby Ranger Charles W. Johnson buried at Lovettsville Union Cemetery – 12930 Lutheran Church Road, Lovettsville
(N39°15′29″ W77°38′16″)**

Mosby Ranger Charles W. Johnson

94) John deButts buried in *Old Welbourne* Cemetery, Dulany Family Cemetery – 21398 Willisville Road, Bluemont (Private Property)
(N39°1′57″ W77°49′23″)

Mosby Ranger John deButts, *Old Welbourne* Cemetery

95) John Mobberly buried at Salem Church Cemetery – 14103 Harpers Ferry Road, Hillsboro
(N39°13′35″ W77°44′24″)

Front and back of John W. Mobberly headstone

The rear of the headstone bears the following inscription which was added by the women he protected:

God bless thee, brave soldier
Thy life dream is o're;
For country and freedom,
Thou will battle no more.

To the land of the blessed,
Thou has gone to depart;
With a smile on thy face,
And joy in thy heart.

Thrice hallowed the green spot,
There our hero is laid;
His deeds from our memory,
Shall never more fade.

The stranger will say,
As he lingers around;
'Tis the grave of a hero,
'Tis liberty's mound.

**96) North Fork Church Cemetery – 38104 North Fork Road, North Fork
(N39°3′36″ W77°41′8″)**

Mosby Ranger John W. Holmes buried at North Fork Church

Mosby Ranger John Kirkpatrick buried at North Fork Church

97) Mosby's Rangers buried at Mount Zion Baptist Church – 40309 John Mosby Highway, Aldie
(N38°57'49" W77 36'44")

Mosby Ranger James Sinclair

Mosby Ranger Jesse McIntosh

Mosby stopped at Matt Lee's house many times during the war **Mosby Ranger William Phineas Thomas**

Mosby Ranger Major William Hibbs

98) Members of the Thirteenth New York Cavalry and the Second Massachusetts Cavalry buried at Mount Zion Baptist Church – 40309 John Mosby Highway, Aldie (N38°57'49" W77°36'44")

Thirteenth New York Cavalry and Second Massachusetts Cavalry Graves at Mount Zion Cemetery

Samuel C. Hanscom, Company A, Second Massachusetts Cavalry. Promoted Corporal and killed in action near Mount Zion Church, Virginia on July 6, 1864. He was shot through the head and lived a few hours until destiny called. He was a member of the California Hundred, from San Francisco, California. He was age twenty-eight years old at enlistment on November 24, 1862.

James McDonald, Company F, Second Massachusetts Cavalry. Promoted to Corporal, killed in action near Aldie, Virginia on July 6, 1864. A miner from California when he enlisted at age thirty years old on June 4, 1864 and became a member of the California Hundred.

Duff Montando, Company H, Thirteenth New York Cavalry. Killed in action near Aldie, Virginia on July 6, 1864.

William F. Dumaresq, Company K, Second Massachusetts Cavalry. Killed in action near Aldie, Virginia on July 6, 1864. He was born in Jersey Island, England. A sailor before the war, he enlisted at age twenty-seven years old on June 1, 1864.

Owen Fox, Company H, Second Massachusetts Cavalry. Killed in action near Aldie, Virginia on July 6, 1864. He was from East Braintree, Massachusetts. A laborer before the war, he enlisted at age twenty-three years old on October 19, 1863. Chaplain Charles A. Humphreys found the mortally wounded Fox pinned under his horse and took him to a nearby farmhouse. It is reported that Fox died that night in terrible pain, crying out to Humphreys, *"Chaplain, they shot me after I surrendered."* Aided by a local farmer with a lantern, and using the farmer's spade, Humphreys was captured while digging a descent grave for poor Fox under a tree near the farmhouse.

John Johnson, Company I, Second Massachusetts Cavalry. Killed in action near Aldie, Virginia on July 6, 1864 only thirty-two days after enlisting on June 4, 1864. He was from Canajoharie, New York. A bricklayer before the war, he enlisted at age twenty-one years old.

Charles Oeldraiher, Company G, Second Massachusetts Cavalry. Killed in action near Aldie, Virginia on July 6, 1864. He was born in Boston, Massachusetts. A tin man before the war, he enlisted at age twenty-two years old on February 29, 1864.

Patrick Riordon, Company I, Second Massachusetts Cavalry. Killed in action near Aldie, Virginia on July 6, 1864. He was from Marlborough, Massachusetts. A shoemaker before the war, he enlisted at age nineteen years old on March 31, 1864.

Charles W. Rollins, Company I, Second Massachusetts Cavalry. Killed in action near Aldie, Virginia on July 6, 1864. He was from Stanstead, Canada East. A farmer before the war, he enlisted at age thirty-eight years old on May 27, 1864.

Cornelius Tobin, Company I, Second Massachusetts Cavalry. Killed in action near Aldie, Virginia on July 6, 1864. He was from Marlborough, Massachusetts. A shoemaker before the war, he enlisted at age nineteen years old on March 21, 1864.

Michael Hubin, Company I, Thirteenth New York Cavalry. His company was formed in Albany, Buffalo and the Watertown area in New York. Killed in action near Aldie, Virginia on July 6, 1864.

Joseph Lovely, Company K, Thirteenth New York Cavalry. His company was formed in the New York City and Brookland area. Killed in action near Aldie, Virginia on July 6, 1864.

99) Arnold Grove Cemetery – 37216 Charles Town Pike (Route 9), Hillsboro (N39°11′53″ W77°42′57″)

Mosby Ranger Ira Follin

100)   Catoctin Free Cemetery 1810-1929 – 39596 Charlestown Pike (Route 9) between Waterford and Hillsboro
(N39°09′50″ W77°38′46″)

Captain Franklin Myers, Thirty-fifth Battalion Virginia Cavalry

**101)   Ebenezer Church Cemetery – 11590 Harpers Ferry Road, Hillsboro
(N39°17′44″ W77°43′11″)**

John Riley, who rode with John Mobberly

102) Hillsboro Cemetery – Charlestown Pike (Route 9) between Hillsboro Road and Mountain Road, Hillsboro
(N39°11′51″ W77°43′6″)

Mosby Ranger Henry R. Moore

103) Ketoctin Church Cemetery – 16595 Ketoctin Church Road, Purcellville (N39°9′26″ W77°44′53″)

T. Clinton Hatcher, Eighth Virginia Infantry

Mosby Ranger Henry Heaton

Mosby Ranger Thaddeus Dowell

Mosby Ranger Townsend Heaton

104) **Lakeview Cemetery – 1891, North Laycock Street, Hamilton**
  (N39°8′22″ W77°39′53″)

Mosby Ranger William H. Fletcher

Mosby Ranger Theodore D. Milton

105) **Saint Paul's Church – 12623 Harpers Ferry Road, Purcellville**
(N39°16′3″ W77°43′34″)

Levi Waters. Ranger Tom Turner would die in his house

106) Sharon Cemetery, incorporated 1849 – 209 East Federal Street, Middleburg (N38°58'09" W77°43'52")

Entrance to Sharon Cemetery

Ranger Charles McDonough, a notorious member of Mosby's command, had a price put on his head after the war was over. McDonough had always sworn he would save the last bullet for himself before he would surrender to the Yankees. On June 18, 1865, McDonough was cornered by the Eighth Illinois Cavalry in Middleburg, and true to his word, committed suicide rather than surrender. He is buried in the Confederate Ring of Honor in Sharon Cemetery.

Mosby Ranger Charles McDonough

Mosby Ranger Thomas W. Adams

Mosby Ranger William A. Brent

Mosby Ranger Benjamin Franklin Carter

Mosby Ranger F. T. Craig

Mosby Ranger Henry Clay Dear

Mosby Ranger G. Y. Dodd

Mosby Ranger Burr P. Fred

Mosby Ranger Frank Lee Fred

Mosby Ranger Dallas Furr

Mosby Ranger Howard J. Gibson

Daniel Hatcher, Major, Seventh Virginia Cavalry. Involved with a fight with Mosby's Rangers. Brother of Harry Hatcher

Mosby Ranger Henry "Harry" Hatcher

Mosby Ranger R. A. Howdershell

Mosby Ranger Thomas A. Martin

Mosby Ranger George K. Pickett

Mosby Ranger Welby H. Rector

Mosby Ranger L. F. Skillman

Mosby Ranger Benjamin F. Skinner

Mosby Ranger George M. Skinner

198

Mosby Ranger Henry W. Skinner

Mosby Ranger William Smallwood

Mosby Ranger Henry H. Smith

Mosby Ranger H. T. Swart

Mosby Ranger Bushrod Underwood

Mosby Ranger John Underwood

Mosby Ranger James W. Waddell

Mosby Ranger J. R. Watkins

107)   Leesburg Union Church Cemetery, established 1855 – 323 North King Street, Leesburg
(N39°11'09" W77°36'29")

Mosby Ranger John M. Adrain

Mosby Ranger John H. Alexander

Henry Ball. Mosby ate at his house on July 5, 1864

Mosby Ranger James Monroe Chancellor

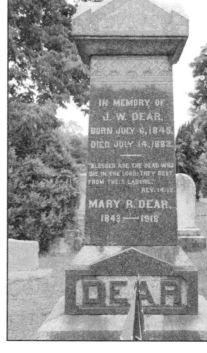

Mosby Ranger Samuel E. Crosen

Mosby Ranger J. William Dear

Mosby Ranger James William Foster. First Captain of Company A, Forty-third Virginia Battalion Cavalry

Mosby Ranger Henry C. Gibson

Mosby Ranger Alfred Glascock

Mosby Ranger John Gray

Mosby Ranger Charles Turner Hawling

Mosby Ranger John R. Hutchinson

Mosby Ranger Thomas W. Hutchison

Mosby Ranger Edgar Jackson

Mosby Ranger Thomas S. Lake

Mosby Ranger James L. McIntosh

Mosby Ranger Charles E. Paxson. Killed at Loudoun Heights

Mosby Ranger George W. Ryon

Mosby Ranger Alexander Spinks

Mosby Ranger Thomas Turner. Mortally wounded at Loudoun Heights

206

Mosby Ranger Decatur H. Vandevanter

Mosby Ranger Dr. Joseph Vandeventer (Note spelling)

Mosby Ranger Townsend H. Vandevanter

207

Field of the Unknown Confederate Soldiers

Colonel Elijah Viers White, Thirty-fifth Battalion Virginia Cavalry

108)   Company A, Loudoun Rangers buried at Waterford Union Church Cemetery – 323 North King Street, Waterford
(N39°11'09" W77°36'29")

Loudoun Rangers Jack W. Virts and William Hough

Loudoun Rangers Charles S. Rinker and John S. Densmore

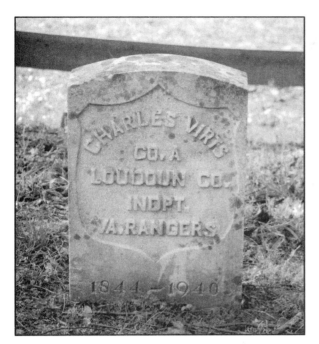 

Loudoun Rangers Charles Virts and Lieutenant Robert Graham

Loudoun Rangers Sergeant Flemon B. Anderson and his father Captain Charles F. Anderson

Loudoun Rangers Sargent J. H. Corbin and Thomas G. Oates

Appendix A. The Almond Birch House

At the end of the war, John G. Viall, the former Captain of the Fifth New York Cavalry, purchased Almond Birch's house. On November 29th, 1865, he wrote a letter to the Governor of Massachusetts stating that there were two troopers from the Second Massachusetts Cavalry buried in his front yard. They were buried under a board grave marker which he could not initially read. Viall's letter is below:

Arcola, Loudoun Co. Va. Nov. 29th 1865
To the Governor of The State of Massachusetts.

SIR:

Since the close of the war I came to this place and purchased the farm from which I now write. On taking possession of the place I found in the yard the graves of two soldiers the names of which had become so nearly obliterated as to be unintelligible. A few days since however I happened to look at the head board during a rain storm when I discovered that the names, etc., had become perfectly plain. I have now seen the former proprietor of the place who informed me that they were killed near the house in a most gallant charge of Mosby's command.

I well remember the gallant and daring affair and so will you Sir, when I add that it was in the effort of a Sergeant and four men to take from Mosby the thirty supply wagons he captured near Fairfax in July 1863 that these men fell. They were buried here by the order and personal supervision of the lamented Lowell and here they can remain but duty to our fallen brave and especially to my brother cavalrymen prompts me to make an appeal to you for a more Christian burial for these men or that their present resting place be so marked that they shall not be at once forgotten.

The inscription on the rough board that now marks the double grave is as follows:

Charles Raymond
H. B. Little
2nd Mass Cavalry
Killed July 31, 1863

I am Governor,
Very Truly, Your Obdt. Servt.
(Signed) John G. Viall
Late Capt. 5th N.Y. Cav.
P.O. Address,
Aldie, Loudoun Co. Va.
Postmaster

Local Loudoun County historian, Wynne Saffer, conducted a land records search and was able to verify that John G. Viall bought his land on the Little River Turnpike from Almond Birch. So these men were buried at the home of Almond Birch where Mosby captured two Union officers late at night on June 17, 1863.

After further research, the authors in consultation with Mosby historian Tom Evans, were able to finally verify that the troopers buried at the Almond Birch house were actually Peter Renard and Hazen B. Little. It turns out there was no Charles Raymond even enlisted in the 2nd Massachusetts Cavalry. The grave diggers at the time carved what they thought was the correct name. However recent research correctly identifies him as Renard.

Shortly after Viall's letter was written, the bodies of the two men were removed to Arlington National Cemetery and reinterred. We can now state that Peter Renard is finally resting in Plot 10413, and Hazen B. Little is in Plot 10305.

John G. Viall was approximately thirty-one years old when he enlisted into Company H, Fifth New York Cavalry, on October 18, 1861 to serve three years as a private. On December 25, 1861, he was commissioned as a second lieutenant and was promoted to first lieutenant on September 16, 1862. On November 7, 1862, Viall was promoted to captain. On May 18, 1864, Captain Viall was mustered out of the Fifth New York Cavalry and was appointed captain and assistant quartermaster, U. S. Volunteers. Major General Hugh Judson Kilpatrick declared that Captain Viall was the *"best quartermaster in the Army of the Potomac."*

Captain Viall died Monday, September 1, 1913, at age eight-five years old. According to his obituary, he fought throughout the Civil War and rose through various stages in the Army of the Potomac to the rank of chief quartermaster. His body was laid to rest in Arlington National Cemetery three days later.

Captain Viall was also one of the few men actually present who saw Major General Philip Sheridan's historic ten mile ride, which started from his headquarters in Winchester, to rally his troops from disaster against a surprise attack by Lieutenant General Jubal A. Early at the Battle of Cedar Creek on October 19, 1864.

Appendix B. Union Lieutenant John H. Black

The story of Union Lieutenant John H. Black, who was critically wounded at the fight in Hamilton on March 21, 1865, is a story during the conflict between love and duty. John H. Black was a schoolteacher who made the decision to fight for his country and leave his beloved fiancée, Susan Jane (Jennie) Leighty, when he enlisted as an Orderly Sergeant in the Twelfth Pennsylvania Cavalry on January 24, 1862. Black's intelligence and education propelled him up the ladder of promotion, from Sergeant to a First Lieutenant in Company G in the Twelfth Pennsylvania Cavalry.

Black spent most of his time throughout 1862 and 1864 in the lower Shenandoah Valley. In early 1864, Black was presented with a dilemma. In order to retain fighting men, the U.S. government offered an inducement of a healthy financial bonus and thirty days leave for any soldier who would re-enlist as a "Veteran Volunteer" for the duration of the war. One side of John wanted to re-enlist despite the extended term of service in order to obtain the quick trip home and thirty days with his beloved Jennie. The other side of him wanted to get out of the army as soon as possible so they could marry and settle down.

On January 3, 1864, Black wrote a letter to Jennie that contained the following:

> *"I will do so (serve) if health and life permits until the 10th of December 1864 [his term of enlistment], and then I will quit soldiering and not re-enlist but will return to my native county and state.... If it were not for you I would have re-enlisted before this. It is for your sake alone that I will forsake a soldier's life... so much I love you, you have often told me in your letters to not re-enlist. And now my dear Jennie, the loved one to me of this wide world, I will solemnly make this candid vow to you. So rest easy, if others do re-enlist, you can safely say that there is one in the Army that loves you so dearly that for your sake he will not re-enlist."*

But the lure of being with Jennie, even for a short period of time, over-came every reservation and his solemn promise. On February 1, 1864, Lieutenant Black re-enlisted.

On March 8, 1864, Black and the rest of the Veteran Volunteers from the Twelfth Pennsylvania Cavalry, commenced their thirty-day leaves and scattered to all corners of the Commonwealth. Jennie and Lieutenant Black made good use of their time and were married in Duncansville during his month home. The time passed quickly and soon John was back with his regiment. His luck held during the first few months of 1865 despite several encounters between the Twelfth Pennsylvania Cavalry and Mosby's partisans. Unfortunately, Mosby would eventually make Lieutenant Black pay for ignoring his wife's wishes that he not re-enlist.

By the end of March 1865, the Twelfth Pennsylvania Cavalry mostly involved in attempting to kill or capture Mosby's Rangers. On March 19, 1865, the majority of Black's regiment went on a reconnaissance-in-force along the Eastern edge of the Blue Ridge Mountains. Mosby was waiting and would spring his ambush in the village of Harmony, Virginia on March 21, 1865.

Lieutenant Black's company was in the vanguard, the forefront of the Union soldiers that day. Despite virtually all of the regiment's officers and men having been fooled over and over by the ploy of the Confederates leaving decoys loitering in the road to feign surprise and panic, the Union troopers once again fell for the bait. With a shout and brandished sabers, the Yankees charged after the Rangers who had been dangled in the middle of the road. After a brief pursuit, both the Blue and Gray entered a stretch of road border by a tree-line. When the Union cavalry were fully committed, the Rangers burst out from behind the trees and into the Union column with pistols cracking and swords hacking into the startled Bluecoats. After a brief but frenzied battle, the Twelfth Pennsylvania Cavalry broke and fled back down the road. Lieutenant Black however was not among his comrades.

Sometime during the fight, one of the Rangers shot Black. He was knocked out of his saddle by a pistol ball that entered at his hip and lodged in the small of his back. Lying in the dust, paralyzed from the waist down, the Rangers stripped him of twenty dollars in cash and his "…hat, boots, jacket, vest, shirt collar, letters, knife, comb, gold pen, and in fact everything but pantaloons, shirt, and drawers…," and then left him to die.

Much to everyone's surprise, including the Rebels who left him behind, Black survived his wounding, but it was too grave to allow for any significant travel. In the first letter he was able to write to his beloved Jennie after being shot. Black described his recovery:

> "I have been at two different houses. The first place I was at was an old lady and her three daughters. They treated me as a mother and sisters would treat a person. I remained there two weeks getting better but not well enough to stand a trip over the river. For fear some rebels might chance along and move me south, I was one night moved to where I now am. Here I am receiving every care and attention that can be given anyone. So do not trouble yourself at all. Just be thankful as I am that my life was spared at all. When I fell from my horse, wounded, I thought my day was sealed…. My wound gives me no pain at all, I rest quite easy…. When the ball struck me, both my legs and in fact all of the parts of my body below the wound was paralyzed. That is what has disabled me so…. My love to you while my name to this as your true, devoted, and affectionate husband…."

Obviously the war was over for Lieutenant Black. Later in the summer of 1865, Black was able to return home to Jennie in Duncansville. Despite his disability, Black returned to teaching, remained an "ardent Republican," and even held the office of county treasurer for three years. Presumably, also because of his war wound, Lieutenant Black and Jennie were unable to have children of their own. Having plenty of love left to share, though, they adopted two daughters.

Sadly, by 1878 Lieutenant Black's life had become a daily ordeal, because he was "…obliged to remain in-doors the greater part of his time, and much of this time he is obliged to spend in bed…. If he remains out of his bed for an hour, his feet become very much swollen, causing him increased pains." Worse, the woman he loved and who stood by him and cared for him despite an affliction that was the direct result of his broken pledge and despite her repeated pleas, passed away in 1908. Fourteen hard years later, the eighty-seven year-old former trooper gave up the pain and the struggle and joined the love of his life, fulfilling his duty both to his country and his wife.

Index

Hibbs, William (Ranger), 62, 143, 144, 183
Hickman, George, 93, 133, 134
Hickman, John, 133, 134, 144
Hill, Frances, 163
Hillsboro Cemetery, 189
Hillsboro, Virginia, 66, 68, 70, 71, 75, 98, 127, 158, 159, 180, 186, 187, 188, 189
Hoe, Mr., 159
Hoge, William, 63
Hollingsworth, Mr., 13
Holmes, John W. (Ranger), 181
Home Guard of Virginia, 6
Hooe, Robert (Ranger), 118
Hooker, General Joseph, 50, 51
Horsepen Run, 27
Hough, Dave, 93
Hough, Henry, 143, 144
Hough, William, 210
Houser, Postmaster Samuel, 6, 7
Houser, Wade, 6
Howdershell, R. A. (Ranger), 197
Hubin, Michael, 185
Humphreys, Chaplain Charles A., 108, 109, 185
Hunter, William (Ranger), 32, 36
Hunton, Colonel Eppa, 8
Huntoon, Captain Franklin T., 29
Hurst, Ned (Ranger), 32, 36
Hutchinson, Thomas W. (Ranger), 204
Hutchison, John R. (Ranger), 204
Hutchison, Lycurgus (Ranger), 42
Ice Cream Raid, 64
Independent Loudoun Virginia Rangers, 17
Ivy Hill Cemetery, 46
Jackson, Edgar (Ranger), 205
Jackson, General Thomas "Stonewall", 45, 150, 154
Jackson, Newton (Ranger), 129
Janney, Asa Moore, 62
Janney, Mr., 159
Janney, Werner, 62
Jefferson County, Virginia, 146
Jefferson, President Thomas, 57
Jersey Island, England, 184
Johnson, Charles, 131
Johnson, Charles W. (Ranger), 178

Johnson, John, 185
Johnson, Joseph (Ranger), 118
Johnson's Chapel, 80, 81
Johnstone, Lieutenant Colonel Robert, 29
Jones, Captain William "Grumble", 1
Jordan, Coley (Ranger), 175
Kabletown, Virginia, 175
Kabrich, Corporal Peter J., 15
Katy's Hollow, 137
Keith, James (Ranger), 138, 140
Kephart, George, 85
Ketoctin Church Cemetery, 190
Key Switch, West Virginia, 146
Keyes, Captain Daniel M., 98, 100
Keys, William, 36
King William Court House, 22
Kirkpatrick, John (Ranger), 181
Lafayette, Marquis de, 57, 91
Lake, Ludwell (Ranger), 88
Lake, Thomas (Ranger), 62, 109, 205
Lakeview Cemetery, 191
Lambert, John, 126
Lane House, 155, 156
Lane, Mortimer (Ranger), 155
Lathen, Wilson, 131
Lee, Frank (Ranger), 195
Lee, General Robert E., 1, 58, 66, 146, 154
Lee, Ludwell, 91
Lee, Matt, 19, 24, 63, 64, 183
Lee, Mrs. Robert E., 161
Lee, Richard Henry, 91
Leesburg and Alexandria Turnpike, 8, 41, 91, 92
Leesburg Union Church Cemetery, 201
Leesburg, Virginia, 6, 13, 26, 32, 41, 57, 76, 85, 87, 88, 94, 95, 96, 97, 103, 104, 105, 113, 121, 124, 125, 126, 154, 174, 201
Leesburg,Virginia, 153
Lenhart, John W., 126
Lewinsville, Virginia, 77
Lewis, Mrs. Joanna, 158
Libby prison, 134
Lincoln, Virginia, 62, 138
Little Big Horn, 141
Little River Turnpike, 20, 22, 23, 25, 28, 29, 32, 42, 46, 50, 64, 105, 116, 155, 161

222

Bibliography

General Sources:

Albaugh III, William A.; *Confederate Faces, A Pictorial Review;* Wilmington, North Carolina; 1993.

Albaugh III, William A.; *More Confederate Faces, A Pictorial Review;* Republished by Broadfoot Publishing Company; Wilmington, North Carolina; 1993.

Alexander, John H.; *Mosby's Men;* Reprinted by the Butternut Press; Gaithersburg, Maryland; Reprint from 1907 edition.

Armstrong, Richard L.; *7th Virginia Cavalry;* H.E. Howard, Inc.; Lynchburg, Virginia; First Edition, 1992.

Armstrong, Richard L.; *11th Virginia Cavalry;* H.E. Howard, Inc., Lynchburg, Virginia; 1989.

Axelrod, Alan; *The War Between the Spies, A History of Espionage During the American Civil War;* The Atlantic Monthly Press; New York; 1992.

Baird, Nancy Chappelear; *Journals of Amanda Virginia Edmonds, Lass of the Mosby Confederacy, 1857 – 1867;* Printed by Commercial Press; 1984.

Beach, William H.; *The First New York (Lincoln) Cavalry, from April 19, 1861 to July 7, 1865;* Published by the Lincoln Cavalry Association; New York; 1988.

Baylor, George; *Bull Run to Bull Run, or, Four Years in the Army of Northern Virginia; Zenger Publishing Company, Inc.; Washington D.C.; 1983.*

Beller, Susan Provost; *Mosby and his Rangers, Adventures of the Gray Ghost;* Betterway Books; Cincinnati, Ohio; 1992.

Bergner, Audrey Windsor; *Old Plantations and Historic Homes around Middleburg, Virginia, and the Families Who Lived and Loved Within Their Walls, Volume II;* Howell Press; Charlottesville, Virginia; 2003.

Boatner III, Mark M.; *The Civil War Dictionary;* Vintage Books, A Division of Random House, Inc.; New York; Revised Edition, 1991.

Bonnell, John C. Jr., *Sabres, Shenandoah, The 21st New York Cavalry, 1863 – 1866;* Burd Street Press; Shippensburg, Pennsylvania; 1996.

Boudrye, Louis N.; *Historic Records of the Fifth New York Cavalry;* Albany, New York; 1865.

Broderbund, Banner Blue Division; *Census Microfilm Records: Virginia 1850;* Family Archive CD 309; Broderbund Software, Inc., 1997.

Brown, David H.; *Renegade Hero;* Unpublished.

Brown, R. Shepard; *Stringfellow of the Fourth;* Crown Publishers, Inc.; New York; 1960.

Bryan, Jr., Charles F. and Lankford, Nelson D.; *Eye of the Storm, A Civil War Odyssey;* The Free Press; A Division of Simon & Schuster; New York, New York; 2000 by the Virginia Historical Society.

Buckland, Eric W.; *Mosby's Keydet Rangers;* That Fateful Night Press; 2010.

Buckland, Eric W.; *Mosby Men;* That Fateful Night Press; 2011.

Buckland, Eric W.; *Mosby Men II;* That Fateful Night Press; 2011.

Buckland, Eric W.; *Mosby Men III;* That Fateful Night Press; 2012.

Buckland, Eric W.; *Mosby Men IV;* That Fateful Night Press; 2013.

Burns, Vincent L.; *The Fifth New York Cavalry, in the Civil War;* McFarland & Company, Inc., Publishers; Jefferson, North Carolina; 2014.

Castleman, Virginia Carter; *Reminiscences of an Oldest Inhabitant, (A Nineteenth Century Chronicle);* Herndon Historical Society, 1976.

Chamberlin, Taylor M. and Souders, John M.; *Between Reb and Yank, A Civil War History of Northern Loudoun County, Virginia;* McFarland & Company, Inc., and London; Jefferson, North Carolina, 2011.

Chamberlin, Taylor M. and Souders, John M.; *A Pocket Guide to Waterford's Civil War;* Waterford Foundation, Inc.; Waterford, Virginia; , 2011.

Civil War Centennial Commission, County of Loudoun, Commonwealth of Virginia; *Loudoun County and the Civil War, A History and Guide*; Loudoun County Board of Supervisors; Loudoun County, Virginia; 1961

Cole, Scott C.; *34th Virginia Cavalry;* H.E. Howard, Inc.; Lynchburg, Virginia; First Edition, 1993.

Collea, Joseph D. Jr.; *The First Vermont Cavalry in the Civil War, A History;* McFarland & Company, Inc., Publishers; Jefferson, North Carolina and London; 2010.

Conley, Brian A.; *Cemeteries of Fairfax County, Virginia, A Report to the Board of Supervisors;* Fairfax County Public Library; 1994.

Connery, William S.; *Mosby's Raids in Civil War Northern Virginia;* Published by The History Press; Charleston, South Carolina; First Edition 2013.

Cooke, John Esten, edited with an Introduction & Notes by Stern, Philip Van Doren; *Wearing of the Gray, Being Personal Portraits, Scenes & Adventures of the War;* Indiana University Press; 1959.

Cooke, John Esten; *Surry of Eagles-Nest;* G.W. Dillingham Co., Publishers; New York; 1894.

Cooling, Benjamin Franklin and Owen, Walton H.; *Mr. Lincoln's Forts, A Guide to the Civil War Defenses of Washington;* White Mane Publishing Company; Shippensburg, Pennsylvania; 1988.

Corbett, Samuel James; *The Civil War Diary of Samuel James Corbett, A Source Book for the California One Hundred;* The Madera Method Historians of Kentfield, Madera, and Modesto, California; The Classroom Chronicles Press, Madera; California; 1992.

Cowles, Captain Calvin D.; by Davis, Major George B, & Perry, Leslie J., & Kirkley, Joseph W. with an introduction by Sommers, Dr. Richard; *The Official Military Atlas of the Civil War;* Arno Press, Crown Publishers, Inc.; New York; 1978.

Crawford, J. Marshall; *Mosby and His Men: A Record of the Adventures of that Renowned Partisan Ranger, John S. Mosby, (Colonel C.S.A.), Including the Exploits of Smith, Chapman, Richards, Montjoy, Turner, Russell, Glasscock, and the Men Under Them;* Invictus; Decatur, Michigan; Reprinted August 1998.

Crouch, Howard R.; *Like a Hurricane, The Men, Mounts, Arms, and Tactics of Colonel John S. Mosby's Command; SCS* Publications; 2013.

Crouch, Richard E., *"Rough-Riding Scout" The Story of John W. Mobberly, Loudoun's Own Civil War Guerilla Hero;* Elden Editions; Arlington, Virginia 1994.

Dannett, Sylvia G.L. and Burkart, Rosamond H.; *Confederate Surgeon, Aristides Monteiro;* Dodd, Mead & Company; New York; 1969.

Daniels, Jonathan; *Mosby, Gray Ghost of the Confederacy;* J.B. Lippincott Company; Philadelphia and New York; 1959.

Davis, William C. and Wiley, Bell I.; *Civil War Times Photographic History of the Civil War, Fort Sumter to Gettysburg;* Black Dog & Leventhal Publishers; New York; Compilation, 1994.

Divine, John E.; *8th Virginia Infantry;* H.E. Howard, Inc.; Lynchburg, Virginia; Second Edition, 1983.

Divine, John E.; *35th Battalion Virginia Cavalry;* H.E. Howard, Inc.; Lynchburg, Virginia; 1985.

Drickamer, Lee C. and Drickamer, Karen D., *Fort Lyon to Harpers Ferry, A Civil War Newsman at Harpers Ferry;* White Mane Publishing Co., Inc.; Shippensburg, Pennsylvania, 1987.

Driver Jr., Robert J.; *1st Virginia Cavalry;* H.E. Howard, Inc.; Lynchburg, Virginia; Second Edition, 1991.

Driver Jr., Robert J.; *First and Second Maryland Cavalry, C.S.A.;* Rockbridge Publishing, an imprint of Howell Press, Inc.; Charlottesville, Virginia; 1999.

Dulany, Ida Powell; *In the Shadow of the Enemy, The Civil War Journal of Ida Powell Dulany;* Edited by Mary L. Mackall, Stevan F. Meserve, and Anne Mackall Sasscer; The University of Tennessee Press; Knoxville, Tennessee; 2009.

Edison High School; *A Hike Through History; Edison High School;* June 1988.

Evans, Thomas J. and Moyer, James M. with a forward by Jones, Virgil Carrington; *Mosby's Confederacy, A Guide to the Roads and Sites of Colonel John Singleton Mosby;* Published by White Mane Publishing Company, Inc.; 1991.

Evans, Thomas J. and Moyer, James M.; *Mosby Vignettes;* Volume 1-5; Printed privately; First Printing February 1983.

Fairfax County Civil War Centennial Commission; *Fairfax County and the War Between the States;* Reprinted by the Office of Comprehensive Planning; Fairfax County, Virginia; 1987.

Fairfax County Historical Society; Historical Society of Fairfax County, Virginia, Inc., Volume 9 – 1964-1965; Published by the Historical Society of Fairfax County, Virginia, Inc.; 1965.

Fairfax County Historical Society; Yearbook: The Historical Society of Fairfax County, Virginia; Volume 26, 1997-1998; Published by the Historical Society of Fairfax County, Virginia, Inc.; 1997.

Fairfax County Board of Supervisors; *Fairfax County Virginia, An Historical Tour Map & Guide to Places of Interest;* Published by the Fairfax County Park Authority in partnership with the Fairfax County History Commission and with the support from the Virginia Foundation for the Humanities and Public Policy; Revised 1986.

Fairfax Genealogical Society; *Fairfax County, Virginia Gravestones;* Volumes 1-6; Fairfax Genealogical Society; Merrifield, Virginia; First Printing 1994.

Forsythe, John W.; *Guerrilla Warfare, and Life in Libby Prison;* Turnpike Press; Annandale, Virginia; 1967.

Fortier, John; *15th Virginia Cavalry;* H.E. Howard, Inc.; Lynchburg, Virginia; 1993.

Frantum, David M.; *Confederate Burials in Northern Virginia, The Final Bivouac of Northern Virginia's "Band of Brothers";* Printed in the United States by the Kirby Lithographic Company; 2000.

Freeman, Douglas Southall; *Lee's Lieutenants, A Study in Command;* 3 volumes; New York; Charles Scribner's Sons; 1942.

Freeman, Douglas Southall; *R.E. Lee, A Biography;* Charles Scribner's Sons, New York; 1934.

Frobel, Anne S.; *The Civil War Diary of Anne S. Frobel;* EPM Publications; McLean, Virginia; 1992.

Gamble, Robert S., *Sully*; Sully Foundation Limited, Fairfax, Virginia, 1973.

Geddes, Jean; *Fairfax County, Historical Highlights from 1607;* Published by Denlinger's; Fairfax, Virginia; 1967.

Gibson, Christine; *Fairfax County Notebook;* Unpublished; No date.

Gibson, Christine and Mitchell, Bill; *The Blaze, Clermont Woods, Clermont – Some Historical Notes;* Published by the Clermont Woods Community Association; Private printing; March 1980.

Glasgow, William M.; *Northern Virginia's Own, The 17th Virginia Infantry Regiment, Confederate States Army;* Published by Gobill Press; Alexandria, Virginia; 1989.

Gold, Thos. D.; *History of Clarke County, Virginia;* Reprinted for Clearfield Company, Inc., by Genealogical Publishing Company, Inc.; Baltimore, Maryland, 1998.

Goodhart, Briscoe; *History of the Independent Loudoun Virginia Rangers, U.S. Vol. Cav. (Scouts), 1862 – 65;* Reprinted by Olde Soldier Books, Inc.; Gaithersburg, Maryland; Originally published 1896.

Guernsey, Alfred and Alden, Henry M.; *Harpers Pictorial History of the Civil War;* Fairfax Press, distributed by Crown Publishers; Originally published in 1866.

Guild Press of Indiana, Inc.; *The Civil War CD-ROM, The War of the Rebellion, A Compilation of the Official Records of the Union and Confederate Armies;* Guild Press of Indiana, Inc.; Indiana; 1996.

Guy, Anne Welsh; *John Mosby, Rebel Raider of the Civil War;* Published by Abelard-Schuman; New York, 1965.

Hakenson, Don and Buckland, Eric; *"Good, Joe! Good for old Company A!" Lieutenant Joseph Henry Nelson, Warrenton, Virginia;* privately published; Unknown.

Hakenson, Donald C., and Mauro, Charles V.; *A Tour Guide and History of Col. John S. Mosby's Combat Operations in Fairfax County, Virginia;* HMS Productions Inc., 2013

Hakenson, Donald C. and Dudding, Gregg; *Mosby Vignettes, Volume VI;* Don Hakenson, 2002.

Hakenson, Donald C. and Dudding, Gregg; *Mosby Vignettes, Volume VII;* Don Hakenson, 2003.

Hakenson, Donald C.; *Reminiscences of Frank H. Rahm of Mosby's Command & An Analysis of Ranger John H. Lunceford: Traitor or Coward? Or Unjustly Accused?;* Don Hakenson, 2008.

Hakenson, Donald C.; *This Forgotten Land; A Tour of Civil War Sites and Other Historical Landmarks South of Alexandria, Virginia;* Don Hakenson, 2002.

Hakenson, Donald C.; *This Forgotten Land, Volume II, Biographical Sketches of Confederate Veterans Buried in Alexandria, Virginia;* Don Hakenson, 2010.

Hale, Laura Virginia and Phillips, Stanley S.; *History of the Forty-Ninth Virginia Infantry C.S.A. "Extra Billy Smith's Boys;* Published by S.S. Phillips and Assoc.; Lanham, Maryland, 1981.

Harrison, Fairfax; *Landmarks of Old Prince William, A study of origins in Northern Virginia, Volumes I & II;* Gateway Press, Inc.; Baltimore, Maryland; 1987.

Helm, Lewis Marshall; *Black Horse Cavalry, Defend Our Beloved Country;* Published by Higher Education Publications; Falls Church, Virginia; 2004.

Historical Society of Loudoun County, Virginia; *The Bulletin of the Historical Society of Loudoun, Virginia, 1957 – 1976;* Published by Goose Creek Productions; Leesburg, Virginia; 1997 & 1998.

Hoadley, J. C.; *Memorial of Henry Sanford Gansevoort, Captain Fifth Artillery, and Lieutenant-Colonel by Brevet, U.S.A.; Colonel Thirteenth New York State Volunteer Cavalry, and Brigadier-General of Volunteers by Brevet;* Franklin Press: Rand, Avery, & Company; Boston, Massachusetts; First Edition 1875.

Hoffman, Elliott W.; *A Vermont Cavalryman in War & Love, The Civil War Letters of Brevet Major General William Wells and Anna Richardson;* Schroeder Publications, 2007.

Hoge, William as told by his son Hoge, Charlie; The Composition Book; Stories from the Old Days in Lincoln Virginia, Told by Asa Moore Janney and Werner Janney; 1987.

Humphreys, Charles A.; *Field, Camp, Hospital, and Prison in the Civil War, 1863 – 1865;* Press of George H. Ellis Company; Boston, Massachusetts; First Edition, 1918.

Hunt, Roger D. & Brown, Jack R.; *Brevet Brigadier Generals in Blue;* Old Soldier Books, Inc.; Gaithersburg, Maryland; Revised Edition 1997.

232

Jacobs, Charles T.; *Civil War Guide to Montgomery County, Maryland*; The Montgomery County Historical Society; Rockville, Maryland; 1996.

Johnson, Robert Underwood and Buel, Clarence Clough; *Battles and Leaders of the Civil War;* Castle Books; New York; Published 1956.

Johnson II, William Page; *Brothers and Cousins: Confederate Soldiers and Sailors of Fairfax County, Virginia;* Iberian Publishing Company; Athens, Georgia; 1995.

Jones, Virgil Carrington; *Gray Ghosts and Rebel Raiders;* Henry Holt and Company; New York; 1956.

Jones, Virgil Carrington; *Ranger Mosby;* Chapel Hill, The University of North Carolina Press; 1944.

Keen, Hugh C. and Mewborn, Horace; *43rd Battalion Virginia Cavalry, Mosby's Command;* H.E. Howard Inc.; Lynchburg, Virginia; Second Edition, 1993.

Kelsey, D.M.; *Deeds of Daring by both Blue and Gray;* Scammell & Company, Publishers; Philadelphia and St. Louis; 1893.

Krick, Robert K.; *Lee's Colonels, A Biographical Register of the Field Officers of the Army of Northern Virginia;* Morningside House, Inc.; Dayton, Ohio; 4th Edition, 1992.

Krick, Robert K.; *9th Virginia Cavalry;* H.E. Howard, Inc.; Lynchburg, Virginia; 4th Edition, 1982.

Lindsey, Mary; *Historic Homes and Landmarks of Alexandria, Virginia;* Alexandria, Virginia; fifth printing; 1944.

Longstreet, James; *From Manassas to Appomattox, Memoirs of the Civil War in America;* William S. Konecky Associates, Inc., 1991.

Loth, Calder; *The Virginia Landmarks Register;* University Press of Virginia; Charlottesville, Virginia; Third Edition 1987.

Maier, Larry B.; *Leather & Steel, The 12th Pennsylvania Cavalry in the Civil War;* Burd Street Press; Shippensburg, Pennsylvania; 2001.

Markle, Donald E.; *Revised Edition, Spies & Spymasters of the Civil War;* Hippocrene Books; New York; 1994.

Mauro, Charles V.; *A Southern Spy in Northern Virginia: The Civil War Album of Laura Ratcliffe;* The History Press; 2009.

Mauro, Charles V.; *Herndon: A History in Images;* The History Press; 2005.

Mauro, Charles V.; *Herndon: A Town and Its History;* The History Press; 2004.

Mauro, Charles V.; *The Battle of Chantilly (Ox Hill): A Monumental Storm;* Fairfax County History Commission; 2002.

Mauro, Charles V.; *The Civil War in Fairfax County: Civilians and Soldiers;* The History Press; 2006.

McAtee, Dr. Kenneth Stuart; *Ghost Stories and Legends from the Confederacy, Volumes 1-2;* Printed privately; First printing September 1993.

McChesney, Carol R.; *Franconia History of the Road;* Unpublished; No date.

McLean, James; California Sabers, The 2nd Massachusetts Cavalry in the Civil War; Indiana University Press; Bloomington, Indianapolis Indiana, 2000.

Meserve, Stevan F.; *The Civil War in Loudoun County Virginia; A History of Hard Times;* The History Press, 2008.

Mitchell, Adele H.; *The Letters of John S. Mosby;* Stuart Mosby Historical Society; second printing 1986.

Moore III, Robert H.; *The 1st and 2nd Stuart Horse Artillery;* H.E. Howard, Inc.; Lynchburg, Virginia; First Edition, 1985.

Mosby, Colonel John S.; *The Memoirs of Colonel John S. Mosby;* Little, Brown, and Company; Boston; 1917.

Mosby, John S.; *Stuart's Cavalry in the Gettysburg Campaign;* Reprinted by Olde Soldiers Books, Inc.; Reprinted in 1987 from a 1908 edition.

Mosby, John S.; *Mosby's War Reminiscences and Stuart's Cavalry Campaigns;* Dodd, Mead & Company, Publishers; New York; 1887.

Moxham, Robert Morgan; *Annandale, Virginia, A Brief History;* Edited by Bryans-Munson, Estella K.; Fairfax County History Commission; 1992.

Munson, John W.; *Reminiscences of a Mosby Guerrilla;* Olde Soldier Books, Inc.; Reprint from a 1906 edition.

Musick, Michael P.; *6th Virginia Cavalry;* H.E. Howard, Inc.; Lynchburg, Virginia; First Edition, 1990.

Myers, Frank M.; *The Comanches: A History of White's Battalion Virginia Cavalry, Laurel Brig., Hampton Div., A.N.V., C.S.A.;* Kelly, Piet & Co., Publishers – Continental Book Company; Marietta, Georgia, 1956.

Netherton, Nan, & Sweig, Donald & Artemel, Janice & Hickin, Patricia & Reed, Patrick; *Fairfax County, Virginia, A History;* Published by the Fairfax County Board of Supervisors; Fairfax County, Virginia; 1992.

Newcomer, C. Armour; *Coles Cavalry; or Three Years in the Saddle in the Shenandoah Valley;* Books and Library Press; Freeport, New York; 1970.

Nichols, James L.; *General Fitzhugh Lee, A Biography;* H.E. Howard, Inc.; Lynchburg, Virginia; Second Edition, 1989.

Northern Virginia Planning District Commission; *Northern Virginia, Understanding and Protecting Our Shared Heritage;* Northern Virginia Planning District Commission; 1981.

O'Neill, Robert F., Jr.; *Chasing Jeb Stuart and John Mosby, The Union Cavalry in Northern Virginia from Second Manassas to Gettysburg;* McFarland & Company, Inc. Publishers; Jefferson, North Carolina; 2012.

O'Neill, Robert F., Jr.; *The Cavalry Battles of Aldie, Middleburg and Upperville June 10-27, 1863;* H.E. Howard Inc., Lynchburg, Virginia; 1993.

Parson, Thomas, E.; *Bear Flag and Bay State in the Civil War, The Californians of the Second Massachusetts Cavalry;* McFarland & Company, Inc., Jefferson, North Carolina, and London; 2001.

Peavey, James Dudley; *Confederate Scout, Virginia's Frank Stringfellow;* Printed by The Eastern Shore Publishing Company, Onancock, Virginia; 1956.

Penfield, James; *Captain James Penfield, 1863 – 1864 Civil War Diary, 5th New York Volunteer Cavalry, Company H;* Press of America Inc.; Ticonderoga, New York; 1999.

Ramage, James A.; *Gray Ghost, The Life of Col. John Singleton Mosby;* The University Press of Kentucky; 1999.

Ramey, Emily G. and Gott, John K.; *The Years of Anguish, Fauquier County, Virginia 1861 – 1865;* Heritage Books, Inc., Bowie, Maryland; 1998.

Ray, William C.; *Mount Gilead, History & Heritage;* Printed by Wert Bookbinding; Grantville, Pennsylvania; 2014.

Records of the United States General Accounting Office. *Records of the Third Auditor, Southern Claims Commission, Fairfax County, 1871-1890;* Record Group 217, Washington D.C., National Archives.

Rogers, Larry and Rogers, Keith; *Their Horses Climbed Trees, A Chronicle of the California 100 and Battalion in the Civil War, from San Francisco to Appomattox;* Schiffer Military History; Atglen, Pennsylvania; 2001.

Rose Hill Civic Association, *The Rambler, Journal of the Rose Hill Civic Association;* Private Printer; June, 1984.

Salmon, John S.; *Revised and Expanded Edition, A Guidebook to Virginia's Historical Markers;* Published by the University Press of Virginia; Charlottesville, Virginia and London; 1994.

Scheel, Eugene M.; *The Guide to Loudoun; A Survey of the Architecture and History of a Virginia County;* Potomac Press; Leesburg, Virginia; 1975.

Scott, Major John; *Partisan Life with Col. John S. Mosby;* Harper & Brothers, Publishers, New York; 1867.

Shosteck, Robert; *Potomac Trail Book;* Bethesda, Maryland; 9th Printing March 1976.

Siepel, Kevin H.; *Rebel, The Life and Times of John Singleton Mosby;* St. Martin's Press; New York; 1983.

Sifakis, Stewart; *Compendium of the Confederate Armies, Virginia;* Facts on File; New York and Oxford; 1992.

Simpkins, Francis Butler, & Hunnicutt, Spotswood, & Poole, Sidman P., *Virginia: History, Government, Geography;* Charles Scribner's Sons; New York; 1957.

Slater, Kitty; *The Hunt Country of America, Then and Now;* Virginia Reel, Inc.; Upperville, Virginia; November 1997.

Sprouse, Edith Moore, *Mount Air, Fairfax County, Virginia;* June 1970.

Stephenson, Richard W.; *The Cartography of Northern Virginia, Facsimile Reproductions of Maps Dating From 1608 to 1915;* Published by the History and Archaeology Section, Office Comprehensive Planning, Fairfax County, Virginia; Revised second printing 1983.

Stepp, John W. and Hill, I. William; *Mirror of War, The Washington Star reports the Civil War;* Prentice-Hall, Inc.; Englewood Cliffs, New Jersey; 1961.

Stiles, Kenneth; *4th Virginia Cavalry;* H.E. Howard, Inc.; Lynchburg, Virginia; Second Edition, 1985.

Stuntz, Connie Pendleton and Stuntz, Mayo Sturdevant; *This Was Virginia 1900 – 1927, As Shown by the Glass Negatives of J. Harry Shannon, The Rambler;* Hallmark Publishing Company; Gloucester Point, Virginia; 1998.

Templeman, Eleanor Lee; *Arlington Heritage, Vignettes of a Virginia County;* Privately published; 1959.

Templeman, Eleanor Lee & Netherton, Nan; *Northern Virginia Heritage, A Pictorial Compilation of the Historic Sites and Homes in the counties of Arlington, Fairfax, Loudoun, Fauquier, Prince William and Stafford, and the cities of Alexandria and Fredericksburg;* Avenel Books; New York; First Published 1959.

Vogtsberger, Margaret Ann; *The Dulanys of Welbourne, A Family in Mosby's Confederacy;* Rockbridge Publishing Company; Berryville, Virginia; 1995.

Wallace, Lee A.; *A Guide to Virginia Military Organizations 1861 – 1865;* H.E. Howard, Inc.; Lynchburg, Virginia; Revised Second Edition, 1986.

Wallace Jr., Lee A.; *17ᵗʰ Virginia Infantry;* H.E. Howard, Inc.; Lynchburg, Virginia; First Edition, 1990.

Warfield, Private Edgar; *Manassas to Appomattox, The War Memoirs of Pvt. Edgar Warfield, 17ᵗʰ Virginia Infantry;* EPM Publications, Inc.; McLean, Virginia; 1996.

Warner, Ezra J.; *Generals in Gray, Lives of the Union Commanders;* Louisiana State University Press; Baton Rouge; 1999.

Warner, Ezra J.; *Generals in Blue, Lives of the Confederate Commanders;* Louisiana State University Press; Baton Rouge and London; 1987.

Wert, Jeffry D.; *Mosby's Rangers;* Simon and Schuster; New York; 1990.

Whitt, James Chapman; *Elephants and Quaker Guns, Northern Virginia: Crossroads of History;* Revised Edition; Vandamere Press, A Division of AB Associates; Arlington, Virginia; 1984.

Williams, Harrison; *Legends of Loudoun, An Account of the History and Homes of a Border County of Virginia's Northern Neck;* Garrett and Massie, Incorporated; Richmond, Virginia; 1938.

Williams, Kimberly Prothro; *A Pride of Place, Rural Residences of Fauquier County, Virginia;* University of Virginia Press; Charlottesville and London, 2003.

Williamson, James J.; *Mosby's Rangers;* Time Life Books; Reprinted 1982 from the 1896 first edition.

Wilson, Gregory P.; *Jonathan Roberts, The Civil War's Quaker Scout & Sheriff;* CreateSpace Independent Publishing Platform; North Charleston, South Carolina; 2014.

Wilson, Gregory P.; *Private John S. Mosby, First Virginia Cavalry, Picketing Fairfax County before Becoming the Confederacy's Gray Ghost;* 2015.

Notes: